LETTERS
FROM THE
LOST SOUL

LETTERS FROM THE LOST SOUL

A
FIVE YEAR VOYAGE OF
DISCOVERY AND ADVENTURE

BOB BITCHIN

SHERIDAN HOUSE

First published 2000 by
Sheridan House Inc.
145 Palisade Street
Dobbs Ferry, NY 10522
www.sheridanhouse.com

Library of Congress Cataloging-in-Publication Data

Bitchin, Bob.
    Letters from the Lost Soul : a five year voyage of discovery and
adventure / Bob Bitchin.
       p. cm.
    ISBN 1-57409-112-3
    1. Bitchin, Bob—Journeys. 2. Lost soul (Sailboat) 3. Voyages and travels.
I. Title.

G530 .B55 2000
910.4'5—dc21   00-036555

Edited by Janine Simon
Designed by Jesse Sanchez
Photographs by the author

Printed in the United States of America

ISBN 1-57409-112-3

This book is dedicated to my mother, Mary, and my father,
S. Marshall Lipkin (may he rest in peace). It is their trust and
confidence that has allowed me to live on the edge all these years.

Introduction

——————————▶◀——————————

I half-felt someone shake me, and for a minute I forgot where I was. As I opened my eyes, I heard Patrick whisper, "Hey man, 10 minutes and you're on."

It was 5:50 in the morning and the sun was about to come up. I walked through the creaking main saloon in the twilight of dawn with the kerosene lights casting a warm glow, and felt the boat heel to port with a little gust of wind. The smell of coffee blended with the aroma of the kerosene, an alcohol stove, and the mildew of a thousand days at sea. As I poured the coffee into my favorite mug, I looked through the porthole and was transfixed. The horizon was a brilliant orange and gold. We were 150 miles off the coast of Guatemala, and that day had the most unreal sunrise I ever saw.

Today, over 20 years later, I can still recall that feeling. The way it felt to walk on deck of the 74-foot square-rigged tops'l schooner STONE WITCH and take the large tiller. The breeze over my shoulder, the telltales whipping, letting me know when to adjust the sails. The feeling of accomplishment, and even more so, pride, as we moved 50 tons of canvas, wood, and steel through the water with just the wind and our sweat.

It's true that you do not change when you go to sea. You are still the same person you always were. The only difference is, for many, it brings out a part of you that you never knew. I have never known anyone whose life was not improved by going to sea.

For some reason unbeknownst to me, many people treat the planning of going cruising as if they were planning to die. They sell their homes, say goodbye to their friends, cancel their magazine subscriptions (aagh! that hurts!), and do every-thing but buy a plot.

Why? They're just going cruising, right? Your life doesn't end when you cut the lines and say *adios* to friends and neigh-bors. Wherever you are heading, someone calls home. That's why cruising is such a great way of life. You get to go out and experience what it's like to live in all types of environments. In Polynesia, you learn to find the ripe fruits for your lunch on trees. In Greece, you can live as people have lived for many millennia. In Antarctica, you can live like a penguin if you want. But the fact still stands, no matter where you go, you are still there. With yourself.

Have you ever met anyone out cruising who is a real grump? You know, the kind of person who walks into a room looking like he smells something bad. Well, you can bet your backup bilge pump he was the same back home. You can't run away from yourself. If anything, cruising introduces you to yourself. There's nothing like a few hundred days jammed to-gether in a vessel the size of a large storage shed, with noth-ing but water surrounding you, to get to know the real you.

Life is just like a cruise. It doesn't matter how or where it ends, it's the journey to reach that end that counts. You have to take every day for what it is. And you will notice that each day you awaken, as you cruise through the world and through your life, you always wake up with the same person. You don't change once you leave. The little things that annoyed you when you were at home will still annoy you. The little thrills you get are the same underway, only better.

The big difference is the joy you get from the small things you never had time to notice. For every cruiser, it's something else. For me, it will always be that feeling I first encountered at 5:50 a.m., March 27, 1978, aboard the STONE WITCH.

*   *   *

For over 20 years I have lived aboard sailing vessels and cruised almost 100,000 miles. In just the past five years I have had the pleasure of sailing some 45,000 miles to the most beautiful places in the world. During this time, I have shouted "I hate boats" a thousand times, sailed with idiots and geniuses, seen poverty and riches, and have been fortunate enough to join the family of cruising sailors—that stupid breed of human that spends weeks at sea in heavy weather, with water dripping into every orifice, and actually has a smile on his face as he enters a storm-swollen harbor. To those who have never done it, you just can't explain what it's all about, and to those who have lived it, no explanation is needed.

I remember well the first morning of the first day that I owned the LOST SOUL. I was disgusted. It was dawn. I'd been up almost all night with anticipation over what I'd do first. My friend Curt came up the 20-foot ladder to the deck as the boat sat on skids in the yard at King Harbor Marine Center in Redondo Beach, California. I was sitting in a glassy-eyed stupor. What had I done? There was no way this would ever be a real boat again. I'd bitten off more than I could chew.

When I first set eyes on what is now the LOST SOUL she was named FAIRWEATHER and had been abandoned for almost seven years. In the previous 20 years I managed to go through no less than six sailboats. I would buy broken-down, forgotten hulks from the backwaters of Southern California harbors, live on them as I fixed them up, and then sell them to make enough to buy bigger and better boats. I started on a 28 Cal and worked my way up through the ranks as I spent 25 years riding around the country in the saddle of a rigid frame Harley-Davidson, working for any motorcycle magazine that would pay me. The names I chose for these boats reflected my somewhat unorthodox lifestyle. You know, romantic names like ROGUE, OUTLAW, PREDATOR, ASSAILANT, and last, but not least, LOST SOUL.

At just a little over 68 feet overall, she is about as big as I think I'd want to go. Officially, she's a 1981 Formosa 56, measuring 56'3" on deck with a 15'8" beam and a draft of eight feet. Eight feet is a bit excessive for a cruising boat, but there's a reason. You see, her first owner had her built by C.Y. Chen over in the Formosa Boat Yard in Taiwan. Formosa was famous for building Bill Garden designed ketches, but some folks complained about the full keel design being too slow. I'd owned two of their 51 footers, and knew how slow they were. We'd lovingly call them Taiwan Turkeys. One enterprising designer, in order to make his boss happy, decided he'd just combine the traditional look of the Garden design with the skag hung rudder and fin-keeled design of a sleek Swan underneath.

Great in theory, but in practice, it left a bit to be desired. After the new owner sailed her awhile he decided he didn't care for the standard rigging. Having more dollars than sense he hustled over to Hong Kong and had all new rigging slung. He added a few feet to the main (now 68 feet to deck), and a few feet to the mizzen (it now takes an Islander 37 tall rig mainsail). He doubled the strength of the rigging by putting no less than 14 stays per mast, and decided not to run a triatic, so if you lose one mast the other will be unaffected. Once again, great in theory—then came the problem.

It seems that after the new, taller rig was in place, the boat was about as tender as a Sabot in a hurricane. Put 15 knots of breeze on her beam and the rails hit the water. On a 42-ton boat that's pretty tender. So he did what any boater with more money than sense would do. He parked it . . . and left it.

Three years later he sobered up long enough to realize that he had left a boat anchored somewhere in Tahiti. He arranged for a captain to bring it back to the States. The captain brought it as far as Hawaii and said he wouldn't sail it any farther. It was too tender.

And so it remained three more years at anchor in Keehi Lagoon, under the takeoff path of the Honolulu airport. The burned jet fuel that fell on it did wonders for the finish. During this time people moved on and off the boat. They stole the sails, took some of the hand-carved teak doors and generally trashed this poor baby. The water started to rise in the engine room, and soon the Ford Lehman engine was covered in salt water.

Once again, the owner came out of a fog and realized he had this boat. He hired someone to bring her home. The guy put a new, less rusted engine in place (this time a new Perkins 135 6-cylinder diesel) and bought some used sails. Three weeks later it was sitting in Ventura Harbor in Southern California, looking pretty sad. Her wood was dried and cracked, and only where the brightwork was buried under things could you see vestiges of varnish.

And that's when this dumb biker stumbled onto the scene. I had just sold *Biker* and *Tattoo* magazines, which I had created and owned for a few years, and was ready to find my ultimate sailing vessel. This was it.

Well, actually, I thought this was it. I haggled for a while and soon was doing the sea trial as we sailed it from Ventura Harbor to Redondo Beach to haul it for a survey. As we sailed it downwind we had a 35-knot wind off our stern, and she hit 13 knots while surfing the Santa Barbara Channel. If there was ever a doubt in my feeble little mind, that cleared it. Of course, I should have gotten the message when the main sheet block gave way, and they couldn't raise the mizzen, but, being a typical dumb-biker-turned-boater, it didn't even phase me.

The next morning, after a friend and I did the survey, I started to assess the damage.

The wiring was all non working, due to it being half submerged while in Hawaii. There was not one piece of working electronics on the boat. The radar actually had cobwebs on the tubes. Been awhile since it had been installed! The 4102 Magnavox SatNav had a broken card, the autopilot was junk, and there were giant cracks in the cap rails where the boat had been hit two or three times. The lifelines hung at various angles from the many bent stanchions and the running rigging did not have one line that wasn't worn through to the core. The cabin soles, though once beautiful, were now so rough they actually absorbed water. At least where there was no oil soaked into them.

I sat there that early morning and realized the truth.

I'd lost my mind!

Curt walked slowly through the boat, not saying a word, just shaking his head. After about 15 minutes he turned to me. "Okay," he said. "Let's go down and hire us some workers to get to work on sanding the wood down to where we can see what it is. Then you should probably pull out all the wiring so you can do it fresh."

He realized that I was so overwhelmed I didn't know where to start. All of a sudden I did. It was that simple, and soon, in less than two hours, I had 13 men who knew less about boats than a desert nomad, and they were sanding with 40-grit sandpaper every wood surface in or on the boat.

Three weeks later I launched the *new* LOST SOUL. I had to replace 28 feet of the cap rail, but the rest was sanded down. We went from 40 to 80 grit, then to 100, and finally to 180. The wood came back like new. I rubbed out the paint, and it started to look pretty good. After repainting the cap and boot strips black, and then the transom for added style, she came alive. I obtained the services of the man who painted the names on the boats at Disneyland's *Pirates of the Caribbean*, and he copied the same style for our name.

The interior was stripped of all cushions and curtains, and we designed all new furnishings. The wiring was redone, the old radar and all other electronics were trashed, and it was starting to look like a real sailing vessel again.

We also added 10,000 pounds of lead to the keel to balance the new higher rig. That was all it needed! Of course, I found out a few months later that the larger keel made it harder to steer with the old rudder, so I had to add 30 percent to the rudder to steer it better, and that overloaded the hydraulic steering ram—so I had to beef it up. You know, whatever you do, you always need to do more.

In any case, after a three-month shakedown cruise to Mexico in 1991 I returned to fix all the things I'd missed the first time.

Chart storage was a problem with so many places to go, so we used overhead, snap-in teak racks for the storage tubes and made a cabinet under the saloon table to hold the rest. It pops up with a door lift from a Toyota hatchback.

When finished it was time to go. We had everything working as well as could be expected, and I was as anxious to set sail as a virgin for her first orgy.

We Go

I had always wanted to sail the South Pacific. You know, dreams of brown-skinned ladies serving tropical drinks as you drift in the clear blue waters. That was the plan. The South Pacific.

In order to truly enjoy a cruise of this magnitude it is very important that you choose your crew well. Being a male of the singular persuasion, I felt the first mate should meet certain, uh, shall we say, standards? Yeah, that's it. Standards. Jody Mason met such standards. You know, the important things. She had been my bartender for quite awhile, was a trained hairdresser (free haircuts!), a masseuse (free massages!) and she had a body to die for! She was immediately signed on as head bartender and chief of protocol.

My friend Andy Arrigali had some sailing experience and was looking for a little adventure in his life, so he was signed on as head womanizer. Jim Zietler, a powerboater, also signed on to go as far as San Diego.

Finishing out the starting crew was a very large, tattooed Captain, aka me!

With the crew all in place, we cast off the lines for the start of our five-year, 50,000-mile adventure.

The first leg is tortuous. Almost 26 miles, to Cherry Cove in Catalina. When we settle in we are greeted by friends who work at the isthmus year-round. An hour after our arrival, VALVOLINE ONE, an 80-mph go-fast boat pulls in with Ronnie and Mike aboard to wish us farewell. We're joined by the 52-foot Pacifica GRAND SLAM and the fishing boat 6-X (Sick Sex). Soon the poop deck of the LOST SOUL is packed with 20 people and munchies are devoured as fast as they are produced. In the evening we make ourselves particularly obnoxious ashore at Doug's Harbor Reef.

We make an overnight stop in Avalon. At 0500 we set sail for San Diego. On the way we discover that the wind meter atop the mast doesn't work. Naturally, it's about the only thing I didn't replace before leaving.

In San Diego we discover:

1. The wind meter can't be fixed.

2. A new one costs $1,000.

3. It is only available in Massachusetts.

4. A rain storm of biblical proportions is on the way into Dago.

5. The solar panels we want to put on the boat are twice the price we expected.

6. We are about to spend three days and $3,000 getting back to sea with our new crew member and new solar panels. The new crew member is John Whyte from England, a furniture maker extraordinaire and our final full-time crew member.

A week later the rain is belting down and the winds are wailing. We drop our lines and head out on the first giant leg of our adventure. We make it almost 12 miles against a 35-knot headwind and 10-foot seas. We decide we are being pretty dumb and spin around to wait for better weather. An hour later we are back at port, sitting in the Kona Kai Yacht Club lounge, downing Sea Breezes and eating luscious prime rib. Four hours out, one hour back. Are we nuts or what?

The next morning the tall ship CALIFORNIAN, tied up next to us at the dock, pulled out. I decided that this was a good omen, and we quickly untied the lines and set out as well. There is nothing like sailing beside a tall ship to instill a real nautical feeling to a crew embarking on a voyage like this. The winds had turned around, and we had a good sail to our first stop in Mexico.

We anchored on the back side of the Coronado Islands, some 15 miles south of San Diego and just across the border in Mexico. We stopped to fix our autopilot, which was doing more wandering than Moses coming out of Egypt, and discovered that our refrigeration system had taken a crapola. After replacing the water pump, we found that the old pump was fine, but that the inverter for the pump was bad. Instead of aborting, we decided just to hot wire the pump and wage onward in the morning. We had planned on lasagna and fresh fish for dinner, but settled on the pasta alone when we couldn't figure out how to divide a one-ounce crab, which was all John caught.

A couple of days later we skirted a pod of whales and headed into the San Carlos anchorage to get out of the weather. The night before we'd pulled into Bahia de San Quintin. Just after we'd set our anchor, a bit after dark, we noticed something. There were very large rollers coming through the anchorage and breaking about 75 feet from where we'd anchored. It took us about as long to up anchor and move as it takes an ant to dance a jig on a hot skillet. Soon we were hunkered in for the night. In the morning we headed south, picking up a couple of bonito and dodging a few more whales. After we anchored I had to go outside and dicker with some local fishermen. Seems they had a few lobsters they could do without, and I had some wine I could spare. A few minutes later John and Andy were cleaning a very large sea bass on deck, and Jody was preparing the lobster in the galley. I sat there playing with my computer, letting the crew do all the work, like a good captain should.

Isla Asuncion is often overlooked by cruisers, which is

why I like to stop there whenever possible. It is a small unin-habited island a day's sail south of Turtle Bay. We motored in shortly after noon and spent the rest of the day exploring the island. Andy had to dive on our prop as the stupid captain (yeah, me) left the trolling line out and it wrapped in the prop.

Punta Belcher. The name itself conjures up images that make it a necessity for the LOST SOUL to stop. It's just a couple miles inside of Magdalena Bay. The wind was blowing 25 knots as we came in. At noon we are anchored next to LADY GUENEVERE and MAGIC CARPET, two boats we'd hopped down the coast with to this point. Keith on LADY GUENEVERE was from England, as is John, our crewman. We were tied up next to him at the Kona Kai Yacht Club in San Diego.

As I write this Andy and John are trying their luck for halibut. We just found out that the great bonito salad Jody made for sandwiches yesterday was in actuality the bait the boys were saving! Yech! We ate bait. Not only that, but we liked it. Everybody is still laughing about that one.

For a couple of days we'd been sitting in Cabo San Lucas in the most perfect weather imaginable. To this point the trip had been as good as one could expect. All we had to do was to get through the next couple of weeks in paradise and we'd be shoving off for French Polynesia. I know, it's a tough job . . .

Powerboats and I have never been close, but in Cabo, sailboats are badly outnumbered. Jody and I went out on SEA MINT, a Bertram 54, to test the engine our friend Clyde had re-built. It seemed odd doing 30 mph on water. Of course, the fuel consumption meter told me we'd used more fuel in an hour than the LOST SOUL used in the two-week sail down, so I didn't feel real bad.

On the night of my birthday we had a bunch of folks off the dock down to the Baja Cantina for a little party. About halfway through our tenth drink I figured the party was going pretty well. There were about a dozen of us there, and we knocked the hell out of a couple of hundred bucks, making John, the owner, real happy, but not doing a lot of good for the cruising kitty, nor our heads the next morning.

Paradise went a little wacky the next few days. Andy flew out to see his mom the morning of the *storm of the century*. We had no idea if he made it to New York or not. He was due back the next day. We also had the old good news/bad news deal. I came down with the flu, that's the bad news. The good news was, Jody had a flu shot before leaving Los Angeles so she was well enough to get me through it. Four days of hell in Heaven.

We took the dinghy out to our own private beach and got some sun and did some swimming in the crystal blue waters. Even being sick is fun down here! I know I should feel guilty about spending my days like this, but what the hell, I'm really out here doing it for you.

So, one night we were down at our favorite watering hole, Latitude 22, and John asked if we might go out for a daysail the next day. He said something about it being Spring break, and there were bunches of young nubiles hanging around. Being a true lover of lasciviousness, I agreed, and told him he could bring as many women as he liked for a little half-day sail the next day.

At ten a.m. the following morning the docks rolled as over a dozen sweet young things came clamoring down the dock looking for us. The crews on all the super-buck, mega-fishing yachts were dumbstruck. I overheard one of them ask John what kind of bait he was using! He nonchalantly answered, "A sailboat."

A few hours later we were anchored off Lovers Beach, surrounded by mounds of female pulchritude, and just loving life. Andy returned from his visit back to New York, and showed up in the dinghy. He couldn't believe all the ladies on board, and soon we were circling the boat, getting lots of photos of the ladies giving us the LOST SOUL Salute.

Oh, you want to know what the LOST SOUL Salute is? Well, it's quite simple. It's like a deep bow, but you face in the opposite direction and pull down your shorts as you do it. You can imagine the ruckus on the beach as a dozen young lovelies gave this "salute" anchored just a few measly yards off the beach. Kodak stock went up that day for sure.

And We're Off

We were sailing on a broad reach, doing about eight knots with 12 knots of wind coming over our port stern. The seas were as calm as a lake, and there were flying fish everywhere. We were about 20 miles off Cabo San Lucas. We'd left at 5 a.m., and the crew had all gone back to sleep. John and Andy had a rough night trying for one last romance before setting sail.

Anyway, we had left for the first leg of our crossing, and I really don't see how it could get much better.

Clarion Island is the farthest island from Mexico and the only stop between North America and French Polynesia. We anchored there during the night. Now there's an adventure, anchoring in a strange port at night with breakers all around. We caught a wahoo on the way and ate like kings.

In the morning we tried to go ashore, but the coast was too rough and there was nowhere to land a dinghy. We finally gave up and decided to stay on the boat. Then we heard some idiots on the radio saying they had taken nine days to sail from Puerto Vallarta (all of 100 miles!), and they wanted to buy fuel and cigarettes on the island on their way to Hawaii. We told them there was no one on the island except about six Mexican Navy personnel, but they kept trying to get them to sell cigarettes and gasoline. They were so obnoxious we decided we would rather head out to sea than chance a visit by these guys, so we bid adieu to Clarion Island. Our next stop should be Nuku Hiva in the Marquesas, French Polynesia.

It started with a bang. I was down in the main saloon spreading out our chart to plot our position. It was noon and the wind was blowing a little over 30 knots. Andy had just gone on watch and asked John what our course should be. Before he could answer, the squall hit us faster than Elizabeth Taylor can down a Twinkie.

The boat veered 60 degrees to port, and our mainsail jibed. As it swung across, with the wind of a full squall, it ripped the preventer and the deadeye on which it was mounted clean out of the deck. It had been held with four ¼ x 20 6-inch through bolts to a stainless mounting bracket on the inside. The sail whipped across the deck with the full force of the wind, and as it hit the end of the main sheet it separated from the eye that attached to the end of the boom, ripping it off. The tension of the sheet ripping apart shot the block back into the solar panels and shattered the one it hit. In a matter of seconds our main was whipping free of any sheets, and we had to run into the wind to drop the sail. As we did, with the full 35 knots of wind on our nose, the boom broke free and knocked Andy off the roof of the storm room. Luckily, Jody was there and as he fell she grabbed at him and they both fell to the deck, just inches from going overboard. We jury-rigged another eye to the boom and put tape on the broken glass of the solar panel. Then the adrenaline started to subside.

The next night we were hit with no less than three squalls, but everything seemed to be holding up. In the morning I awoke to clearing skies, the winds down to 15 knots, and, generally, it was a cleanup day after the previous day's disaster. We were exactly halfway from Cabo to the Marquesas, 1,332 miles in either direction to hit land.

We were 300 miles above the equator and other than a bunch of squalls around us we were having a pretty good crossing. Actually, a couple of days ahead of schedule, but that could change at any time. During the midnight watch we were hit by something I'd never experienced before. We were doing about seven to eight knots under 15 knots of wind off our stern quarter, when all of a sudden a squall came up. After a few minutes, Andy had to get up and help with the wheel, as the autopilot wouldn't do its job. Anyway, about 30 minutes into this screaming meanie something grabbed a hold of the boat and knocked her flat on her side. All of a sudden we were looking at the world from an all new perspective—lying on our backs. No "Excuse me" or "Hey buddy, would ya mind?" just a full-on knockdown with the boat lying over on her side for a couple of seconds.

Of course the sleeping crew below was real happy about this. John was buried under a pile of porno magazines (strictly for trade with the natives, he claims), and Jody had about a hundred books pile themselves, not so gently, on her head.

I wound up lying against the inner wall of the storm room, and Andy ended up atop the steering wheel. During this little two-second knockdown we lost a couple of jugs of fuel over the side, but they were tied on so we retrieved them. We broke a couple of lines that held the dinghy in place, the chart tubes on the upper saloon bulkhead took a walk, and a coffee cup was broken. But we lived through it. Once again, we're on our way south.

As we were about to cross the equator, the weather was perfect. It was so beautiful, I almost felt guilty. On the midnight watch there were more stars out than at the Academy Awards, and sunup was the most beautiful sunrise yet. We would soon stop at the equator to start a new LOST SOUL tradition.

Equatorial Delirium

———▶◀———

We had a party on the equator. So as not to be type-cast doing the same old Shellback Society initiation, we came up with our own. Each crew member holds a hard-boiled egg in his/her mouth and dives in, right on the equator. Then we toast with champagne.

It was so calm that we didn't even bother to put down our steadying sail. Each person popped a hard-boiled egg in their mouth, and dutifully was shoved overboard by a large tattooed captain. When I was the last one standing on deck I popped an egg in my mouth and dove overboard also.

Now let's talk about stupidity, shall we? Here we are, literally thousands of miles from land in every direction, and old El Stupido has everyone on the ship overboard, with the sails up. Brilliant, huh?

Anyway, Poseidon must have been busy, for he did not bring in the winds to blow the boat away and teach us a lesson. It stayed put, and I sat there treading water about 75 feet from the boat, looking back on it, and marveling that we had actually sailed her across the equator.

It also started to enter my feeble little mind that there are some really weird things that live this far from land. All of a sudden I felt very vulnerable just dangling my feet downward into a dark abyss that held multiple-headed demons, and I stroked it for the boat. I have to admit I felt a whole lot better once aboard. We opened the champagne that we'd saved just for this occasion, and toasted our entry into the Shellback Society. I even handed out certificates that I'd made up on the computer for just this occasion.

It was just about then that we discovered that our rudder

had stopped working. Lovely. Here we were, literally in the middle of nowhere, and no rudder! We got to have fun and games on the equator fixing a broken bolt on the rudder post. I was just glad it didn't happen while we were in a squall.

Land Ho!

———————►◄———————

*A*fter 18 days and 2,700 miles we make it to the Marquesas. We arrive in Nuku Hiva at dawn. I took John along with me to translate, as he said he spoke some French, and we went in to do our clearance. By the time we anchored in the bay and made our way to shore to do the paperwork it was 10:30 and the *gendarmerie* had already closed. We had to wait until 2:30, so John and I go over to Maurice's (a small local store) and grab a case of Hinano Beer (just under $60 for a case of beer, including deposit!). It is cold and good. A little later we go back in. It is here that I discover that John's French was learned in school in England, and is a little closer to Greek when heard by the Frenchman who is checking us in. But we've done it. We are finally in the land that cruisers' dreams are made of.

In the evening we find our way up to a little place on a hill overlooking the bay, run by an American lady named Rose. We make it our official home away from home here in Nuku Hiva, and every night we have Happy Hour. Now here comes a real "small world" story. On the fourth evening Jody and I are having a cocktail with Rose. She's talking about a boat in which she and her late husband sailed around the Pacific. As she describes it I realize I know the boat. Not only that, but I had met her and her late husband while I surveyed it for a couple of friends of mine who were buying it from them in San Diego, four years earlier. Yeah, it is a small world.

As we sat talking with Rose, we watched a large, what looked like a cruise ship, enter the bay below. It was the VIRGINIAN, a 203-foot Feadship belonging to John Kluge.

A couple of launches were put in the water, and a bunch of folks disembarked and headed for shore. A few minutes

•-•

later a van pulled up outside the inn, and they started to file in. I kind of recognized an elderly gentleman, but couldn't remember from where or when. I get that a lot (Yes, I lived through the sixties!). In any case, they soon asked us to join them, and I found that the elderly gentleman was Alex Photenhour, previously the captain of HIGHLANDER, Malcolm Forbes boat. In a previous life I was the publisher of *Biker* Magazine, and had met him when I was riding with Malcolm, who was an avid motorcycle rider, about eight years earlier.

It seems that his son, Ingo, was the captain of the VIRGINIAN, anchored below. We started talking and I wheedled an invite to check out what a powerboat should be. She was built a few years ago and is just plain unbelievable. You could put the LOST SOUL in her engine room without removing the masts! On her stern deck are more toys than in Toys "R" Us. She has four galleys, five washers and dryers, more glassware than a department store, and $250,000 worth of frozen meats in her freezer. She also sports a two-ton marble bathtub, and ceramic tile floors in the heads that cost over $200,000 each.

A few days later John, Jody, and I sailed to a small place about four miles west, called Daniel's Bay. Andy had gotten lucky the night before and never made it back to the boat. We figured we'd catch up with him later in the afternoon. Daniel's Bay was an unbelievable little hidden harbor around a bend so well protected you couldn't see it until you were about to enter it. It was like something out of a movie. It had two little bays, one with a white sandy beach and palm trees, the other the same, but with a small river coming out through the rocks. After being introduced to a new fruit called pamplemousse, which I fell in love with, we commenced to motor our dinghy up the river, until we hit a rock and busted the damned prop. Then we hiked six miles through a rain forest to see a waterfall. All the way, as we trudged through waist-deep water, slimy mud and eel-infested pits, I kept saying to myself, it can't be worth it.

I was wrong. As it turns out this is the second highest waterfall in the world. The only higher one is in Venezuela. When we reached the falls, located about dead center on the island of Nuku Hiva, it was overpowering. The water drops about 1,000 feet into a pool. When we swam out into the water falling into this hollow cone it pushed the air through with so much force it threw spray up like it was raining in a wind tunnel. The walls around the canyon shot straight up until they were lost in the clouds overhead. Birds lazed in circles in the updraft, and we were surrounded by banana trees, large mangroves, and giant ferns. All around the waterfall were small piles of stones left by natives after some ancient religious rite. I don't think there is a place on earth I have ever felt so close to God. The pathway to the falls, which was difficult to find, passed six or seven ancient rock altars, and you could see traces of an old civilization everywhere.

When we got back to the boat we found that the prop on the dinghy was now pretty useless. We tried to repair it but the rubber bushing was gone. The dinghy wouldn't do over four knots.

On sailing back to pick up Andy we found that our friend Neil McNeil had flown in by way of Papeete and found a small plane that made a once a week trip to Nuku Hiva. He would sail with us from here to Papeete.

We tried to find a new prop for the dinghy, or a way to fix the bushing, but had no luck. We were bummed. A few days later we departed to explore the rest of the Marquesas.

Ancient Lands and No-See-Ums

*U*a-Pou. The name conjures up ancient Polynesian cultures. It's about 26 miles from Nuku Hiva and at least a hundred years away. There are five pinnacles that reach up into the clouds, and at least one is shrouded in clouds all the time. The island is less than half the size of Catalina and is overgrown with green. To describe it as Bali Hai from the movie *South Pacific* would be appropriate. We land in a small bay (we are the only sailboat) and go ashore to try and clear in. The village has about 50 people. We met one old Marquesan, and he invited us up to his house, where we met his daughter, son, son-in-law, grandson, and another man whose relationship to the family we never did figure out. They gave us some bananas and a dozen pamplemousses, big brother to our grapefruit. It is juicier, sweeter, and much larger—and it's green! That night we made drinks from them and this morning ate them for breakfast. They are unbelievable. Later today the folks are coming out to the boat. We are going to give them rope, perfume, and candy and toys for the little one. They didn't have a prop anywhere on the island. Meanwhile, they were catching some fish for us. This is only the second island, but it is by far the better one. The people don't speak English, or even French. They speak Marquesan, which is harder to understand than a teenager's motives.

Last night goes down as one of the bad times. It started when we'd left Ua-Pou at dawn, heading for Hiva Oa. It was to be a 65-mile day trip, and as we headed around the windward side of the island we found the wind was blowing 25 knots right on our nose. It was the South Pacific trades, but they'd shifted from northeast to southeast. We started to motor into it. A while later our bilge pump alarm went off, and we discovered our bilge was filled to trip our deep water alarm. For the next hour John and I played electrician, discovered the switch was bad, and then played replace-the-bilge-pump-switch while the boat bounced up and down into the seas. Some time later we were hit with a couple of big squalls, which we now call Neil winds, because we know he caused them. Soon we got used to them, so when they'd hit us we'd strip down and shower in all the fresh water they dropped.

It was starting to look like we still might make it into the bay we'd chosen in daylight. Then we got hit by stronger winds, so we picked an alternate bay, called Hanamenu, on the north side of the island, and headed for it. Of course, the wind shifted right onto our nose again. Then the high-temp alarm on the engine went off. A little digging found we'd thrown a fan belt, stopping the water pump. We'd cooked the water out of the engine faster than a forgotten teapot. Once again it was into the engine room (over 150° in there) to change fan belts. This put us just far enough behind to where there was no way to get into the bay by dark.

Now if there's one thing I hate more than pulling toenails with a pair of pliers, it is entering a strange bay after dark. Not only that, but by the time we got to the entrance of this little (less than ¼-mile wide) bay tapering to about 200 feet, it was dark, rainy, overcast, and the spotlight started screwing up. It took a bit, and I had to steer in from the lower steering station, blind except for the radar. Add to that a small squall, and it's about as enjoyable as seeing your young daughter enter a biker bar.

Once in, we set our anchor, had a dinner of filet mignon, and, coming out of shock, giggled like school kids. In the morning it looked a lot less foreboding, and there was a coconut plantation at the head of the bay, with overhanging cliffs on both side. Quite nice.

We made a quick, one-night stop in Hiva Oa, which was so far our least favorite island, due to overcrowding and a generally dirty harbor, and we motored across the bay to Tahuata Island. There we found the idyllic beaches you dream about. We anchored in a small bay with no name and no people. At the head of the bay was a white sandy beach with coconut palms; on one side was a small beach with fruit trees growing down to the water's edge.

While checking out the beach John discovered coconut crabs in profusion, and soon a hunt ensued. John and Neil waited until just before sunset to go ashore and hunt for our dinner. This proved to be particularly bad timing. First of all, Neil speared himself in the foot while landing on the beach, and then it seems that in areas where fresh water sits in tropical climates, you get all kinds of bugs. This particular island was known for its no-see-ums. Little mini-mosquitos that, when they bite, leave a welt the size of Dolly Parton's best known assets. John's back looked like he had the pox—well over 500 bites. Neil got off easiest with about five or six; the rest of us had 30 to 40 spaced evenly over our bodies. I tried to eat one of the little crabs that they'd given quarts of blood to retrieve, but after tearing off the little claws and cracking them open, all I could find was enough meat to fill a gnat's butt, so I gave up.

Due to the overabundance of no-see-ums, we decided this wasn't the place for us, and headed farther south.

We came upon the most beautiful place we've seen yet. It's half a mile from the Hapatoni village and is surrounded by crystal blue waters and mountains covered with rain forest. Rain forests? This should have been our first clue. Rain forest: rain! And it did. We stayed there all day, and it never stopped. We had a very wet crew, with mosquito bites, a speared foot, and damp dispositions.

When we arrive at Fatu Hiva, we are greeted by what has to be the most beautiful little valley on any island in paradise—tall spires with white birds circling over a dark green rain forest and deep blue waters. We anchor at about 2:30 p.m., and a little after dark three outrigger canoes pull alongside and ask permission to come aboard. Six young men, ranging in age from about 16 to 28, come aboard with guitars and Marquesan mandolins, and proceed to sing for the rest of the night, all Marquesan songs. They are all tattooed, so I feel right at home.

While they played I filmed them with my video camera. After a while I invited them down below to watch themselves on the TV. It never dawned on me that they had never seen a television set.

They sat grinning as they watched, and then all of a sudden one of them realized he was looking at himself. He freaked! He started jumping up and down and pointing, and when the others realized they were there too, well, to say it was a moving evening would be an understatement.

By the end of the night they've promised to show us a waterfall the next day, and to help us find some fruits for our sail to the Tuamotus. Oh, and we asked if they might have a prop for our still injured dinghy, but no luck. I was starting to think we'd have to explore the Tuamotus without a motor on the dinghy!

While we stayed in Fatu Hiva we had been adopted by the six young men. We spoke no Marquesan, and they spoke no English, but they'd hang out on board the boat all day, taking advantage of store-bought cigarettes and "citified" munchies. The next day they did show us the waterfall, which was as beautiful as the one in Nuku Hiva, only in a different way. Then we were invited to their homes where we found Meniko's mother had an infected foot, so we went out to the boat and got some cleansers and dressings, and while some of us munched on fish they had made, Andy played doctor. Later we gave them some rope for their outriggers and some per-fume for the girls, and they loaded us down with lots of fish, fresh pamplemousses, green oranges, limes, and papayas.

One day John got out his hair clippers and they all wanted haircuts. There were no barbers on the island. Jody gave them the latest in civilized haircuts.

After about a week it got to where they would show up the first thing each morning, and wouldn't leave until we forced them to leave so we could go to sleep at night. It was almost with a sigh of relief that we departed for our next leg, sailing to the Tuamotu Archipelago.

Heaven Turns to Hell

W e were finishing a 500-mile crossing that had been one for the books: four days and three nights of a 15-knot wind off our stern at about 120 degrees. We never even had to change our sails, except a few times when we wanted to go a little faster and ran our spinnaker. We were about 30 miles off Manihi, which has its highest point at about 60 feet. And that's the top of a palm tree. The first one to spot it got a cold beer . . . so I went topside.

Andy got the beer. He climbed the mast about 15 miles from the island and spotted it. As we got closer, we saw it was just like we'd been told it would be. Just a white sandy beach surrounding a blue lagoon. Getting into it was a lot of fun. As we found out later, we were real lucky. We entered the pass, at high tide, just by accident. As we got through the end of the pass our depth sounder was reading 7'6". Since our hull is eight-foot deep, that's enough to put the fear of God into an atheist.

We worked our way over to a small motu of white sand and palm trees. We were all anxious to get the hook set and go for a swim, and to explore the motu. Andy and John swam off to a small bay, while Jody, Neil and I swam straight into the beach.

As we walked this most beautiful motu, picking up shells and just kind of marveling at the fact that places like this still exist, we heard a shout from Andy and John.

I didn't know if they were being attacked by sharks, or being attacked by the natives. We ran toward their direction, and John was running in front, waving something at us.

It was a prop for a 25 horsepower Johnson outboard,

which is what we'd been searching for over a month. He'd kicked it as he was going ashore. The prop was a little tweaked, but the rubber bushing was good. We rushed out to put it on, and the dinghy worked fine. We had a functioning dinghy once again.

We hoisted anchor a little later and headed over to a small picturesque hotel. Small white cabins sitting on stilts with blue roofs over crystal clear waters. This place was right out of a travel brochure. After downing a breakfast that some-one else cooked, we decided we could put up with a little schmaltz for awhile. For the next two days, we ate hotel food, used hotel docks, and generally made like hotel guests. When we left we were presented a genuine hotel bill, for about $500, and that was just for food and our bar tab. The bill was taped to our refrigerator to remind us to eat on board. But as we were anchored in the next little motu called Ahe, about five miles south, the shock of the bill had passed. Once again we were anchored in a paradise.

Ahe is a smaller atoll, about four miles in diameter. It's a strip of white sand with palm trees surrounding a multi-colored blue lagoon. Getting in was a little hairy, as the en-trance was six feet deep over the bar, with just a very small, maybe 10-foot area, that was eight feet deep. The water was like crystal, and the beach pure white sand, so we went for it. Once in we worked our way into a tight little anchorage. We went ashore when we got the anchor set, cracked a coconut, and toasted the most beautiful island we'd seen. Of course, since we were anchored among a bunch of coral heads, I planned to sleep like a long-tailed cat in a roomful of rocking chairs.

Aaaagghh!!! There are SHARKS out there! Yeah, I meant to use all capital letters, because these were capital-sized grey sharks. John, Jody, and I went out with the dinghy to do a drift-dive in the pass. That's where you dinghy out to the far end of a pass and jump in, letting the current take you through the beauty of the reef. As we drifted through the pass into the lagoon, we started to see some sharks. No big deal as we'd been swimming with white tip, black tip and nurse sharks since we'd been in the islands. We were kind of used to them. But all of a sudden we started to see real, man-eater types.

At first there was just one or two coming out of the depths at the end of the pass. By the time there were seven in view, I was climbing into the dinghy, with John right behind. Jody was about 30 feet away, and was not moving. She was frozen by the sight of the sharks coming up at her. We motored over and I pulled her out just before the sharks reached her. Then, just to show what dunderheads we really are, we decided to shoot the other side of the pass. Brilliant, ain't we? On the second pass we all hung pretty tight to the dinghy as we drifted through the clear waters. Near the end of the pass we saw about eight or nine large sharks near the bottom again, so Jody and I were in the boat about as fast as a rabbit running from a forest fire. John, being British, and trying to be cool, kind of hung there . . . until he turned around and saw about ten more rising up to him. At that point he was also making like he had ants in his skivvies. In all we counted twenty sharks before we left the area for good!

The best laid plans of mice and men oft go astray, and so it was with our departure from Ahe. It began in the afternoon when the wind started to come up, and all of a sudden, the cute anchorage with all the nice dive spots turned into the anchorage from hell, with coral heads all around trying to take bites out of our hull. As the wind built, we hurried to haul anchor, and just barely got out before we would have drifted onto one of the larger and sharper coral heads. We found our way out of the anchorage and headed across the lagoon to the pass.

We searched for the deepest part of the entrance with John and Neil on the bow. They watched for coral heads or low water. They watched as we entered the pass. They watched as we headed over the low bar. They watched as we headed onto a reef, and they watched as we went aground!

It seems they were discussing if it was deep enough before telling me they weren't sure. It wasn't. We hit. Hard! The current helped to push us over the bar and dragged us clear, taking about an inch of fiberglass off the bottom of the keel. There is nothing quite like the feel of your boat heeled over 15 degrees and the sound and feel of coral dragging across the hull. The rudder didn't touch, and after we were out of the pass everything seemed to work okay, so we headed toward Rangiroa.

By 3:30 a.m. we were off the entrance of Rangiroa bouncing around in a storm. Now I like entering a strange anchorage at night about as much as Zsa Zsa likes Beverly Hills cops, so we tacked back and forth for the next two hours waiting for daylight.

Rangiroa is as pretty as the other Tuamotu islands. There are about 200 shades of blue in the water, and the anchorage is well protected. It is the third largest atoll in the world, 40 miles long and 26 miles wide. We ran into a couple of crew members, one from Denmark and the other from San Francisco, who needed to go to Papeete. We offered them a ride, and took off after a couple of days when the winds subsided.

Huahine was an overnight sail from Moorea. The first few hours of the overnight, 85-mile passage went as smooth as a frog's hair. Eight to ten knots of wind off our beam driving us at six knots. Then, as usual, Mother Nature decided she'd like to give us a bit of grief, so she did, in the form of a squall. It lasted all night with heavy rains and winds up to 40 knots. Just about as much fun as passing peach pits! At dawn we were about five miles from Huahine and were glad to get in and anchor.

The next evening, Andy and John decided they would try to drink the island of Huahine dry. Before they did, they became intoxicated enough to run the inflatable up on a reef until it dug an 18-inch hole in the bottom. When they reached the boat they were knee-deep in water, and couldn't figure why. Then Andy dropped the handheld radio. In a matter of a few minutes, my $5,000 dinghy and $350 radio were history.

We awoke this morning in Huahine and realized that Andy had left the boat during the night. He had taken a return ticket I had bought as a bond that was needed for each crew member, packed his bag and never even said goodbye. After the ripped dinghy and dropped radio, I guess he felt bad.

Typical Day

*I*t comes to mind that I have not really covered a typical day on an island in paradise. As we drove around Raiatea it came to me just how foreign a way of life it would seem if I were back home. As we left Huahine, we could see Raiatea and Tahaa across the 26-mile channel. Then, as we were sailing across, we saw Bora Bora rising in the distance, another 18 miles farther on. When we entered the lagoon that surrounds Raiatea and Tahaa, we headed to the Moorings Marina, where we picked up a mooring. In the morning, we rented a car. It was raining and we needed some supplies, so we headed to town, and then drove around the island. As we drove, we watched the side of the road for certain trees. We got a stalk of bananas off a tree on the south side of the island, and then found a good papaya tree with some almost ripe fruit. When we stopped at a beach to check out a small island that was about 25 feet around (no kidding) and had three palm trees growing on it, we saw some coconuts and grabbed them. The only thing we didn't find was any pamplemousse trees, and they are my favorite, but tomorrow is another day. After we drove around the island we headed into town to watch the start of an around-the-island bicycle race. Then it was back to the boat, where Jody made cookies and the rest of us kicked back and read. It's a tough life out there.

Tahaa is, as I know you have heard me say before about almost every island, the best island we hit so far. It is everyone's ideal of a South Pacific Island. A small island surrounded by a reef with small atolls of white sand and palm trees, complete with the deepest colors of blue and green you can imagine. We anchored off a small island called Vahine Island. It is owned by a Frenchman who stopped cruising and bought it, and run by Charles, another Frenchman and a sail boat captain by trade. It's idyllic, with the bluest, greenest water you have ever seen and a couple of good moorings, along with excellent food and a view of Bora Bora that is hard to beat, especially at sundown.

It's time to go out and do a little snorkeling, and then we have to sail about five miles to our next anchorage, a small bay that overlooks Bora Bora and have a lunch of papaya, pamplemousse and breadfruit with cheese. Are you sure I have to go home some day?

I was worried that Bora Bora would be a letdown. After all, all my life I've been told it's the most beautiful island in the world. It is everything it has been rumored to be. A hundred shades of blue and green, unspoiled by high rises. It has friendly people and good anchorages. We pulled into the Bora Bora Yacht Club after a 15-mile downwind sail at well over eight knots. The passes getting out of Tahaa and into Bora were both real nerve tinglers. Breaking waves and you have to hope the charts are right. Leaving Tahaa was the most nerve-wracking, 15-foot breakers a hundred feet on each side of you. A boater's worst nightmare. But I have to admit, it did add a little adventure.

One evening we were having dinner at Bloody Mary's, which is a most excellent dive, with dirt floors and a list of customers that reads like a who's who. Rick, the manager, invited us to go with him for a little shark feeding and diving expedition on Sunday. Sunday morning in a blowing squall we loaded up the old dinghy and headed out. The trip to the other side of the island was about like riding a bucking bronco in a rainstorm. The waves broke over the front of the dinghy and the only dry spot on the boat was where our butts clinched the rubber of the dinghy. It was so wet I couldn't see to steer the boat. Then I got a brainstorm. A minute later, I had my diving mask on with the snorkel upside down so I could breath, then the others got the idea and put theirs on. Now picture this, five grown people with their snorkel gear on, roaring around Bora Bora in a dinghy from hell. It looked like a very wet Martian invasion.

As we came around the south side of the island it got *shallow*! Like about one or two feet deep, for about two miles. We alternated between motoring and pulling the dinghy like Humphrey Bogart in some demented scene out of *The African Queen*. We finally got into deep enough water to motor again, and then we had to cross a reef to meet them for the shark feeding.

Now folks, let me ask you this, what kind of a dunderhead gets into a rubber boat and goes over sharp coral that can make your boat go "pop" where there are a hundred or so sharks in a feeding frenzy? Anyway, as we pried the boat off the reef, thanking whatever deity there is that we didn't actually go pop, we turned around and headed back to the beach of a small island, to discuss among us just how stupid we really were. Then, to prove it, we decided to head on around the rest of the island in the dinghy. Eight hours later, blistered by the sun, every muscle in every body so sore you couldn't move, we made it back to the boat. There was not a dry shirt, towel or body on board, and the dinghy looked like we had just been through Hurricane Mitch. In the morning, our bodies felt like we had just finished the second day of Marine Corps basic training. I was so sore even my hair hurt.

We headed over to a safe harbor on the south end of Tahaa. We spent two glorious days doing nothing but getting sun and reading. Then we went to Raiatea to pick up my friends Keith Ball and Toby. Keith has been the editor of *Easyriders* for the past 27 years, and Toby is from Massachusetts. I've known Keith for 20 years, and when I started to plan this trip it was when he and I were sailing over to Catalina for a weekend. The original plan was for him to join me for the whole trip. Then he was to sail with me for three or four months. Then it was 10 to 15 days. He finally came, and stayed for six days.

In order to teach him it isn't nice to screw with my plans, while he was here I ran him through the paces. We started when he missed the connections from Papeete to Raiatea and came in on another flight. I missed him at the airport, but he found his way to the boat. We loaded their stuff onto the boat and gave them a 15-minute 50 mph tour of Raiatea. Then we departed for Tahaa, and back to the Vahine Island resort, which has become our second home. That night we supped on the finest meal we'd had in awhile and in the morning we struck off for Bora Bora. There we showed Keith and Toby no mercy. We ran 'em over to the Yacht Club and forced them to drink mass quantities of Hinano, the local brew, and then dragged them off in the dinghy to a small atoll for snorkeling. Back to the boat for a sunset drink, and then over to the yacht club for dinner. By the time we returned to the boat, they were exhausted.

At dawn, we woke 'em up and threw them into the dinghy. This time for a whirlwind tour of Vaitape, the small town on Bora Bora. After a half hour of "leisure" sightseeing, we dragged them back aboard the boat, and we shoved off for a little daysail.

We started by sailing out of Bora Bora's reef, across the channel to Tahaa and into the reef there, across the reef-strewn channel between Tahaa and Raiatea, and out the other side at Raiatea. We passed Huahine as the sun was setting, and through the night we watched the two of them vie for the better position at the rail for precision projectile spewing.

Toby won with the best toss of the evening. For the rest of the trip across, 100 miles directly into a 20-knot six-foot sea, they stayed in their bunks, while Jody and I fought the seas. About halfway we watched our brand new mainsail disintegrate. A small tear appeared near the top, and a few minutes later the sail was little more than a rag hanging from our mast. We got it down and settled in for a rocky-rolly trip. Then we smelled something burning. Our transmission! We managed to motor the rest of the way and at ten the next morning, we arrived in Moorea. Our transmission was toast.

I pickled the overheated tranny in motor oil while Keith and Toby started to recover. Finally they got what they wanted. Two days of rest and relaxation. Moorea is one of the nicest stays in Tahiti, and we made the best of it, but first thing Saturday we were off again, motoring to Papeete. There we got to play transmission mechanic for a few hours, took them to the quay to eat Chinese food from the side of a truck, and shipped them out, complete with a bag of ripped sails, to Los Angeles at two a.m. via Air New Zealand. I don't know about them, but I sure needed a rest after they were on the plane.

New Crew

W e found two new crew members to sail with us, Joel and Luke from Canada, ages 19 and 18 respectively. They had taken a little vacation after graduating from high school up in British Columbia. They hitchhiked to San Diego, where they met a man who was leaving to sail to Papeete and needed some help. They signed on, and, living on a menu of peanut butter and Coca-Cola, sailed from Mexico to Tahiti. Once there they were left on the beach to fend for themselves.

They met a lot of cruisers, and worked on a few boats in exchange for a place to stay and food. They heard that we were looking for crew for a section of our trip, and they'd put out a radio call on the single sideband radio net. Word got to us in Bora Bora, and we made arrangements to talk to them by radio. After we got some references, we signed them on.

Finding a mechanic to repair the transmission was a pretty tough thing to do. I could just picture going to a marine diesel mechanic who speaks nothing but French, and me speaking nothing but English, and trying to explain a leaking seal on a shifting fork in a Borg Warner transmission on a Perkins 135 Diesel. I took my trusted Sony video camera, turned on the lights in the engine room, and video'd the engine while it ran, complete with leaking transmission, and a touch of directorial skill by having Jody point to the leak with a screwdriver. All very professional. Then we got in our dinghy and headed over to the mechanic's, where I thrust the video into his bewildered hands. He looked startled for a second, and then started to smile. His head bobbed up and down, and finally he got a big grin on his face, handed me back the camera, and said, much to my pleasure, "No problem."

A few days later, we were anchored in Moorea getting ready to barbecue steaks and have a Caesar salad. The only drawback we'd had was that the mainsail we had made for us did not come back with our friends Curt and Jill, and we had to sail without a mainsail for a week, from Papeete to Bora Bora, a trip of about 125 miles.

At night we left Cooks Bay in Moorea and things looked pretty bad. Strong winds, heavy rains. We even had to put up our storm room. Of course then the rain stopped and the weather cleared. It was great. As we were about to enter the reef at Tahaa, our fishing line started to sing.

We caught a marlin. Really! The first ever marlin caught on the LOST SOUL. We backed down on it just like a real powerboat while Curt reeled him in. A little over 45 minutes later we gaffed and pulled on board a black marlin weighing between 150 and 200 pounds. That evening we moored off Vahine Island while Charles and Evelyn prepared a marlin feast that looked like a scene out of a Roman orgy.

We enjoyed another week in our home away from home, Bora Bora, and had a great time with our friends Curt and Jill. But they had to fly home, and it was time for us to head out in search for more adventure. Our new sail arrived from Los Angeles aboard a special flight, and we hanked it in place.

That night we bid adieu to the crews of the VIRGINIAN, OSPRAY, MOONPATH (from South Africa) and SILVER EAGLE (from Poland) at a little party, and we departed Bora Bora the following morning under fanfare befitting a true cruising yacht. With the music of John Philip Sousa blasting from our loud speakers, we hoisted our brand new mainsail, and headed out the pass to the west-northwest. As we pulled out we thought we might have to put up our spinnaker, the wind was so light. Did we turn out to be wrong!

Hell night started about two hours after we left Bora Bora.

It was 4:30 p.m. and we were watching Maupiti approach on our port. We were about 12 miles away, and the sun was just setting. All of a sudden I noticed a tear in my brand new mainsail. I couldn't believe it. I stared open mouthed and soon Jody wondered why I was catching flies with my mouth. When she saw it she just hung her head, I swear I saw a tear in her eye. Joel and Luke were the next to notice it, an 18-inch tear about three feet below the second reef point in our brand new sail.

I decided it would be better to reef while in the rocky-rolly waves we were in, instead of waiting until we were in the lee of the island where it would be calm, but dark. We pulled the sail down to its second reef point, just above the tear, and secured the sail. Now I was set to sail the next 1,500 miles to Samoa, where I could fix it, with a double-reefed main. As it turned out, it was a good thing we did reef it then. Just after the sun set the wind started to blow like a freshman hooker. Before long we had 35-knot winds off our butts, and the boat rocked and rolled. As the night wore on, the winds grew. About midnight I decided to head for Mopelia, so we changed course. With our double-reefed main and reefed headsail we did eight to nine knots in the now 35-knot winds. By sunup we had 35-45 knot winds and were 20 miles from the island. We were sure to be there by 11 a.m.

Until the %&$%#@# wind shifted. It shifted right off our nose. A full gale out of the southeast, with 15-foot seas, and we were motoring into it to get there and to relative calm waters. As we approached the island we were hit by a big mother of a squall, complete with heavy rain, but we arrived undaunted and started to search for a pass. When we found one we wished we hadn't. The water was running out of a 30-foot wide pass at over eight knots! As we approached I was going to try it, but it would have been sheer insanity. About 50 feet from the edge of the reef I turned the LOST SOUL around, and heard my crew start to breathe again.

When you think it's as bad as it's going to get, old Mother Nature throws the book at you. We sat the night at anchor watch, anchored in the lee of this island. The winds were howling from 35 to 55 knots and started to shift out of the northeast. All of a sudden, the boat started to rock like some demented baby in a rocker on speed. We turned on the single sideband radio only to find out there was a large front headed our way, and the way we would know it arrived would be when the winds started to come around from the north, and then the 40- to 45-knot winds would shift to the northwest. Of course, there was one direction that the wind would put us onto the reef. The northwest!

Time for Final Exams

———————————►◄———————————

*S*o here we sat. The boat was rocking, the pass had waves breaking across the opening, and there was a storm on the way that would have us going straight into it for 750 miles to our next stop. This was the final exam of sailing as far as I'm concerned.

Young Luke and I jumped into the dinghy and fought our way through the waves to the pass to check it out again. It was gushing through the pass at about seven to eight knots, with large breakers across the front and a lot of very shallow coral heads on the inside. The winds would be blowing at 45 to 50 knots on our beam if we tried to go through. We took the dinghy to the other side of the island to see if we could anchor there, but the waves from the southeast storm were still breaking at about 15 feet there.

Okay, so here were our choices on this final exam we were facing. We could:

1. Stay where we were and get thrown on the reef, and die;

2. Try to get through a 30-foot wide hole in a reef with a six- to eight-knot outward current, large breakers on the outside, and shallows on the inside with a 40-knot crosswind, and die;

3. Anchor on the south side to hide from the northwester, and get thrown on the reef by a 15-foot south swell, and die; or,

4. Sail into a full gale off our nose for three or four days, and wish we were dead.

We decided to opt for door number 2. I tied some weights from a weight belt (Jody's idea) to a line and knotted it at nine

●-●

feet. Then Luke and I jumped back in the dinghy and fought our way back into the pass. We tested it and decided if we could stay between the coral heads at the back side of the pass, after getting through the breakers and the narrow pass, and not get blown into the reef by the beam wind, we could make it.

Without thinking I went back to the boat, instructed the crew what to do if/when we hit the reef, took two Xanax, said a small prayer (first time in years!), and we hauled anchor.

A squall appeared on the horizon as we started into position, but by then we were committed. As we approached the pass, I tested to see how high I could rev the engine safely, and going into the seas and winds I could get her up to eight knots. With Joel hanging tight on the spreaders, Luke on the bow pulpit, Jody on the video camera (we had to get this one on film!), and a sweating, nervous captain behind the wheel, we turned into the pass. I almost swallowed my tongue as the current swept the bow away from the entrance like King Kong picked up Fay Wray. I fought for control and got her back headed into what now looked like too small a slip with very fast running water and a surfers' paradise in front of it. We caught a wave that was breaking and I wondered if it would wash us up onto the reef, but it didn't.

Even though we were doing close to eight knots, when we started into the pass it looked like we were standing still. Only I was spinning the wheel like in some demented scene from an old *Tugboat Annie* rerun. The current just rushed through, and once in the entrance of the pass it looked like we had about six to eight feet on either side of the boat to where it was about a foot deep. As we got about 100 yards into the pass, it narrowed even more, but it was 20 feet deep under us. I kept whistling the theme song from *Gilligan's Island* and wishing I had Ginger on board.

There was no turning back, so I just kept it pointed straight as I could. The beam wind kept pushing us to the starboard side, and soon we were within two or three feet of the reef. The outward current was running at about 7½ knots; you could have crawled faster than we were moving. In what seemed like an eternity, we were clearing the deep fast-running current, and were now in water that looked to be about deep enough to stand in, but the depth sounder said 10 feet. We dodged between coral heads with Joel still on the spreaders and Luke still on the pulpit, and now Jody was re-laying messages since the howling wind made it impossible to hear. Then, all at once, we were in the clear and deep (40-60 feet) water of the lagoon. I looked behind me and from this side it looked like it was about 12 feet wide. Getting out will be another story. I guess if it was easy, everyone would be doing it, right?

We motored across the lagoon into a safe anchorage and were soon greeted by some local divers. Here on Mopelia they farm black pearls and dive for fish. As I wrote this, Luke and Joel were out with them being shown where to dive for fish. We would probably be sitting out the storm here (since we couldn't get out now if we wanted too) for about four days. It could be worse. The lagoon is beautiful, the atoll is like back in the Tuamotus, and the people are friendlier than any we have met so far. Unfortunately, they don't speak English, and very little French (they speak a Maupiti dialect of Polynesian), but we are getting along very well with hand signals. We are 260 miles from Papeete, 1,200 miles from Tonga, and about as far from civilization as one can get, and we love it!

We stayed in Mopelia for about five days and fell in love with the place. The locals adopted us as extended family and showed us around the motu, took us fishing, lobstering, and showed us how to get heart of palm for salads. In all, there are about five families that live spread out on the motus. We laid on mile-long virgin white sand beaches in clear, blue waters and watched the storm waves break on the outer reef. We explored motus and visited small bird islands where thousands of terns lived. We picked up tern eggs for our breakfast and literally lived off the land with eggs, lobster, fish, heart of palm and coconuts.

Let There Be Light

A bout a year before our arrival this island had been hit hard by a hurricane. The highest point of land on the atoll is about eight feet, not counting palm trees. When the hurricane hit the storm surge was over 12 feet.

You got it. The highest point of land was four feet under water. Prior to that there were about fifteen families living there. They had dogs and cats, chickens and pigs, and an occasional goat.

When the storm hit the people climbed the palm trees and tied themselves to the trees.

Unfortunately about half the trees didn't make it. Half the population of the island was wiped out. Now there were just four families left on the island, and no dogs, cats, chickens and pigs.

Our new friend Igor and his family that we were visiting had found some batteries and solar panels which were left in what remained of the French weather station that used to be there. Of course they didn't know how to use them. That afternoon I went out to the boat and made some little lights from some extra bulbs we had on board. I just soldered short pieces of wire on the bulb contacts. Then we brought in some extra wire, and after cleaning up the panels and hooking up the batteries we managed to get lights into one of the huts.

That night we felt a real glow as we sat aboard having dinner, watching the glow of the light in their hut. Talk about your warm fuzzies!

But all good things must end, and when the weather let up we figured it was time to head on our way to our next stop, Suvarov Island.

After talking with another boat that was leaving Bora Bora

that day, and asking them to bring some supplies for our friends, we hoisted anchor at high noon so we could see our way around the coral heads as we tried to dodge our way out of the pass. We didn't realize it at the time, but when we'd come in against the current we were actually working under a great advantage. As we did eight knots through the water, we were only doing a couple of knots over the ground, so it was easy to see and dodge the coral heads. All of a sudden it hit me. On the way out the current would be with us. We would be pushed through on a current running about six knots. Since we had to do a minimum of four knots to maintain steerage, we'd be doing 10 knots over the bottom. Unfortunately we'd be steering in slow motion, at the speed of a boat doing four knots.

As we broke out of the pass we were hit head on with some breaking six-foot swells. Made Luke hang on pretty tight as we broke into the surf, as he was standing on the bow pulpit watching for coral heads. Joel was pretty safe, up on the first spreader.

Just as we were clear we saw Igor and his friends coming out in a small boat. They wanted to say goodbye. They came aboard and presented each of us with a shell necklace. They'd stayed up most of the night making them, and were still asleep as we were hoisting our anchor. Saying goodbye was a very difficult thing to do, knowing we would probably never see them again.

The next four days we sailed to Suvarov (Suwarrow) Island. During the passage, Luke attained the highest point score possible on watch. He managed to get a rogue wave to break against the side of the boat, causing 70 to 100 gallons of cold saltwater to come straight down the aft hatch at two a.m. on top of where Jody and I were sleeping. Have you any idea what it's like waking up to the gush of cold water on your head and the splish-splash of fish in your bed with you? You don't want to know!

Suvarov

I have wanted to come to the island of Suvarov for years. I had heard this story about a man named Tom Neale who wrote the book *An Island to Oneself*. He lived there as a hermit for years until his death in 1976. The cabin is still here, and now the island is a national monument for the Cook Islands. The caretaker for the past five years is a 65-year-old man named Ioane Kaitara, and he couldn't be more hospitable. There is also his wife Mama Ioane, his grandson Teira, about 10 years old and who prefers to be called Samson, and Jessie, Ioane's son. He got the bends while diving when his nitrogen regulator exploded in New Zealand. The only other resident is a cousin, Takipo, who is the best coconut tree climber you've ever seen.

"When you visit our island you are family," Ioane would say, "and family eats together." Every night we would eat together.

For every night we stayed in Suvarov, they had a barbecue for us and any other boaters that came in. No charge, just lots of coconut crabs, lobsters, fish, and breadfruit. During the day they would invite us to dive with them, or go fishing, or to visit the outlying motus. We would fish, or dive, and catch what we'd eat that night for supper. Of course we would bring in canned fruits or vegetables, but they didn't need them. They made some of the greatest tasting food from the plants found right on the island.

One night we had tuna, served whole on a banana leaf, the next night lobster, broiled on an open grill. One evening we were treated to barbecued frigate bird. During the day Ioane and his grandson took Luke and Joel out to the motu where the frigate birds hung out. Ioane gave each of them a stick, and told them to swack a couple of birds each over the head, and give them to him. He said he'd do the rest.

Luke had a problem with swacking a helpless bird over the head, when it would just stand there and look at him. Ioane told him "Go ahead, do it!"

So Luke took the stick firmly in hand and gave a re-sounding smack to the nearest bird, with his eyes held shut. Ioane picked up the bird, twisted its neck, and looked at Luke, smiling. "Thou shalt not kill," he grinned.

Luke just looked a little dejected, and went to get another bird. That night we dined on three frigates apiece. They tasted like chicken, but a little salty.

We spent our days exploring unvisited motus and swimming on pristine beaches on small palm covered white sand islets. One motu we found we named Bathtub Island, because on the surf side, about twenty yards up from the surf line, there was a natural bathtub formation in the coral.

Ioane and I could sit for hours and discuss the beauties of life, and the things of importance, and have a perfect understanding. This amazed me. An aging ex-biker and an old man who'd never seen television, feeling like kindred spirits. Different backgrounds, but equal values.

One night, I asked him if we could repay him in some way for his hospitality. He smiled and said that the appreciation he could see in the eyes of our crew was more than payment. It seems that in the true Polynesian culture, the thing that makes a person get a good feeling inside, "warm fuzzies," is to do something for others. The fact that he can help another person makes his day.

Those in the civilized world seem to get the same feeling from knowing they have bested someone, or taken advantage. The simplicity of the life on these "uncivilized" islands makes what we'd lived with at home seem gross, crass, and almost criminal.

As we lived in that society, all that we'd left back home seemed unreal, like a bad dream, a nightmare. Now that we have returned to civilization, what we lived out there seems to be a dream. But a good one. One we yearn to return to.

And that is the difference.

If there was just one day, one hour, that had more effect on me than any other in my life, it would be one day I spent on Suvarov Island.

I'd taken the dinghy early in the morning, and headed five miles across the lagoon, to a small atoll on the western reef. The water in the lagoon was crystal clear, and I could see the reefs and teeming sea life below. When I reached the small atoll with just one little palm tree on it, I felt like Robinson Crusoe must have felt as he discovered his island. I don't believe anyone had set foot on it in years. The single white tern living there came out to greet me, and stayed hovering over my head as I wandered around this private paradise. When I sat down on a large, sun bleached piece of driftwood, with my feet in the water, he landed about three feet from me and walked right up to me, as if to say, "What's up?"

No fear, just curiosity. I sat there looking to the sea, and the tern stood beside me. Two friends just enjoying the moment, and each other's company.

Exhilaration, pure and simple. That was the feeling that filled me almost to bursting. For the rest of my life, when I want to recall what it means to cruise, I will remember that moment.

I don't know why we ever left, but leave we did.

Land of the Giants

As we left Suvarov, the winds were light and out of the southwest, as they were supposed to be. We caught a 30-pound yellowtail and were looking forward to a sashimi dinner. Half a day later, the winds were blowing at 25 to 35 knots off our beam, and the seas were building. By that night, the winds had gone up to 40 knots and the seas were untenable. They were breaking over the boat and it was, to say the least, uncomfortable. All night they built, and then at 4:30 a.m., on Jody's watch, the steering started to get almost impossible. We all tried taking turns but the boat just couldn't be held on course. The autopilot wouldn't do it and neither could we. Then we heard a loud snap. The rudder post had broken loose. Now the boat was turning into the wind, as sailboats will do, and we had no control. The seas were well over 15 feet and breaking. Then we heard another loud pop; this time it was our mizzen sail, which had backwinded when we lost our rudder, and blew out. So Jody and Joel brought down the torn mizzen, while Luke and I got to play "fix the rudder." Now if you ever want to get a lesson on how to get seasick, try standing on your head under the aft berth with a wrench in each hand as the seas rock the boat in every direction. After about an hour the steering was re-connected and we started to move again. For about ten minutes. Then the autopilot took a poop.

Once more back under a berth (why are all hard things to fix under berths?) and another half hour of fix and play. So here I was, up all night, no sleep, slamming waves and heavy seas, a couple of hours with wrenches and things, and I had still managed to hold on. And then the bilge pump decided to take a poop too. I got to try standing on my head in the bilge, filled with all kinds of slimudgeons and slimerlions, not to mention giant bilge slugs and slime monsters. The boat rocked and rolled, and finally it was fixed too. We won't go into how the forerunning lights quit, or the gas gauge on tank one, or the rudder position indicator. Let me just say that this, more than any before, was the night from hell.

As we approached the island, once again the weather gods decided to puke on us. Twenty-five-knot winds, high seas, and, as we came within five miles of the mouth of the harbor, rain so hard you couldn't see the front of the boat. We had to enter under radar. Once inside, we knew we had made a mistake. The harbor was full of sunken and half-sunken freighters, filthy fishing boats and a flotilla of cruising boats, covered with slime.

Samoa is the land of the repressed giants. Just how large are these folks, you ask? Well, I'm 6'4" and weigh in at a little over 330 pounds, and I have to shop in the petite section, that's how large *they* are. And there is little doubt how these folks got this way. The food here is to-die-for. Our favorite place has turned out to be Sadie's. It is the original Sadie Thompson's, which was once a whorehouse. No wonder I feel so at home! Anyway, the cook is a Samoan named Sualua who trained at La Costa in Southern California. The man's Beef Wellington is ambrosia of the gods, and his rack of lamb gives goose bumps and shivers of delight. Down the street is Paisano's Pizza. Once again, the best.

It is a little repressive however. You are not allowed on the street between six and six thirty p.m. because that's prayer time. If you are on the street these three to four large Samoans use you for batting practice. Men must wear either long pants or a lava lava, and women must cover from ankle to neck. In a land where the average women weighs in at a good 400 pounds, maybe that's a blessing.

Sometimes the world seems smaller than a flea's rectum. About five years ago a couple who are friends of mine, John and Paitra, untied their boat, ALACRITY II, from their dock at the Portofino Inn in Redondo and sailed off into the sunset with their dog Bonehead and their cat. I knew they were here somewhere and was not surprised to hear they had been living in Pago Pago. I talked to them on the radio and we are planning to meet them in Vava'u, Tonga, next week. They've left Pago Pago to help raise a boat that sank about 180 miles south of there, on Niuatoputapu, a small island of the Tonga group. The boat they went to raise was a 105-foot steel three-masted schooner called GOLDEN DAWN that I was negotiating to buy before I found the LOST SOUL. I had been up to Oxnard to inspect GOLDEN DAWN three times, and was really bummed when I couldn't come to terms with her owner. I ran into her again in Catalina with the new owner on board, and heard of his plans to sail her to the South Pacific. Now here I was, just 180 miles from where she met her demise, with friends of mine, who don't know I almost bought her, working to salvage her.

One weekend they held the Samoa Cup finals at the Pago Pago Yacht Club. We attended the three days of eating, partying, eating, racing, eating and, oh yeah, munching. In three days they went through about five barbecued pigs, a hundred or so pounds of sausages, chickens, taro root, breadfruit, coconuts, salads, and a few hundred other goodies. I used to wonder why Samoans are all so big, now I know. They ate so much I started to think I was anorexic.

After a week in Pago Pago being filled with Samoan food and drink, we set sail for Vava'u, Tonga. Of course being true Lost Souls, first we had to kidnap a young damsel named Ali. Ali is a cute young blonde we first met at the Samoa Cup finals. She was wandering around with a kind of lost look in her eye, and since she was attractive and adventuresome, it only seemed right that she take off with us. The next thing she knew we were clearing customs and sailing off into three days of the most perfect sailing we have encountered this trip. Perfect 15-knot winds off our beam and smooth seas. The autopilot handled it all, and Ali still thinks that's what sailing is like. Boy, did we have her fooled!

Back in the Vava'u group of Tonga we discovered what a cruising paradise would look like had it been designed by Walt Disney. Hundreds of great anchorages, pristine white small sand islands with emerald waters and coconuts dropping at your side to quench your thirst. Tonga is still an unspoiled cruising ground. The Bounty Bar sits on a hill overlooking the bay and is the unofficial home for the sailor far from his home. They not only serve up a great cold beer and hamburger, but their VHF radio is on all day to transfer messages, act as a contact, and be the social center for the cruisers.

For 10 days Jody, Ali and I, along with the crew of Joel and Luke, sailed from one deserted island paradise to another. Of course, when you visit the more popular dive spots or anchorages you can be among other cruisers, but if you want to get out there and be alone, there is no problem. The snorkeling and diving are unsurpassed. There are living reefs with colorful coral and sea life at most of the anchorages. At Mariner's Cave, you can dive to the entrance at about eight feet and swim through a 14-foot tunnel to a brilliant blue grotto. This was a real gut wrencher for us lilly livers. The hole was big enough, but the first time you swim that 14 feet into the cave you feel like it's more like 50. Jody bumped her head as she came up, and once you are inside the cave every time a wave hits the air inside pressurizes to form a green mist. For the less adventuresome you can dinghy into Swallows Cave which has an 85-foot ceiling.

One of the best experiences on the islands is the Tongan feast which has been produced for 20 years by Aisea at Lisa Beach. It is a feast with lobster, fish, lamb, vegetables, and all kind of delicacies laid out in true Tongan fashion. You sit cross-legged on bamboo mats and eat with your fingers, but that didn't even slow down the LOST SOUL crew, and we managed to devour everything that was piled in front of us. Then there was an authentic Tongan dance festival.

In the main village of Nieafu the men wear skirtlike tupanu or lava lavas, and the women wear decorative waist-bands, called ta'ovala, tied with belts made from coconut fibers over their grass woven skirts. It is only recently that singing and dancing have been allowed on Sundays in Tonga as the Church had forbidden this for years. The women still swim fully clothed as do most of the men. While visiting the village, long pants are requested for men, and it is against the law for a man to go without a shirt.

One evening Luke and Joel decided to go over to another boat and play a little poker. This left Jody, Ali and me to our own devices aboard the boat. It could be worse.

As I was laying on the cushion on the aft deck, I remember thinking life couldn't get much better than this. The sky was clear, there were a million or so stars above me, Nat King Cole was serenading me over the outdoor speakers, and it was a beautiful night. The fact that there were two lovely young women with me didn't hurt the evening at all.

That night, as the wine flowed, so did any repression. By midnight any fantasies of mine that had been unlived to that point were achieved, and surpassed.

It seems that part of the reason Ali and her boyfriend had separated was because of a little lack of, shall we say, carnal knowledge? Jody was able to show her what she had been lacking. You might call it a little pre-marital training.

In the morning Luke and Joel were more than a little surprised as the three of us walked out of the aft cabin.

We went ashore for breakfast and Ali couldn't wait to call her ex and tell him what she'd learned. In a few hours she was on a plane home to Pago Pago, and they were soon married.

That afternoon we made plans with our friends from Redondo, John and Paitra, to have dinner. While there we met their boat guest, Kari. She needed a ride back to Pago, and we were heading back there in a little while. She would sail with us.

It was time for us to head out to find the final resting spot for GOLDEN DAWN and see what trouble we could get into elsewhere.

Fun and Games in Pago Pago

*T*he crew for this leg consisted of one large, tattooed captain, one well-endowed first mate, Jody, two deck slaves, Luke and Joel, and our newest kidnappee, Kari. We finally made it out of Vava'u and headed north to Niuatoputapu Island, which is the northernmost island in the Tonga chain. On the way out of Vava'u, another seam let go in our new mainsail. This was almost a record, as the last tear happened leaving Bora Bora, at two hours out. This one lasted two and a half hours after we'd gotten it fixed in Niafu by the sailmaker from the yacht JACARANDA. We sailed the rest of the way to Niuatoputapu under a reefed sail, which was slow going, since we only had 10 knots of wind. That was just part of the fun. About halfway, we noticed our bilge pump going off excessively. Kari came up with a quizzical look on her face. "Uh, there's water running down below. Is there supposed to be?"

A quick check showed we were taking on water from a one-inch hole in our main engine exhaust system. I went to shut down the through hull only to learn that the gate valve was stuck. I tried to shove a rag in the one-inch hole. It then became a three-inch hole. It seems that the galvanized elbow had rotted through from the inside. Now we were taking on water faster than a Jewish mother takes on guilt. In fact, more water than our 3,000-gph bilge pump could handle. No problem. I turned on our secondary emergency bilge pump. This could almost handle it, but just to be safe I figured I'd check the hand bilge.

Oops. No handle. Forgot to get one before I left home. Oh well, no problem, we still have the three-inch-high pressure emergency gas-powered bilge pump. Except we loaned our last gas to a man in a small boat who was out of fuel as we were leaving Vava'u. So we had no gas.

The next 10 hours were spent in deep prayer. I turned on the engine to lessen the water leaking in. With the engine on, it was just the exhaust water coming in (and filling the boat with exhaust so we all had to stay outside). If I shut the engine down the water came in a three-inch gush. Too much for the bilge pumps. If it had become a problem we could have shut down the engine and plugged the exhaust from the outside, and sailed in with no problems. I just like to make it sound hairy for literary purposes.

We made it into Niuatoputapu and spent the day repairing torn sails, fixing exhaust elbows (isn't West epoxy great stuff?), and kicking back.

We met the folks who were raising the GOLDEN DAWN, and found out they had raised it that day almost to the surface, only to have a line break, and the boat settled back to the bottom again. They didn't think it would be up for another three or four weeks.

We decided to head on up to Apia, Western Samoa. The sail there was uneventful, until we turned east to go the last 20 miles into the harbor. The wind gusted up to 25 knots, and the seas kept us down to two and a half knots for ten hours to get into the harbor. After we dealt with some extremely obnoxious customs people, we cleared in and settled down at anchor. It seems that the day we arrived was the start of the big Samoa outrigger races, and these folks take their racing seriously.

For the next week we watched canoe races and went sightseeing around a really beautiful island. We slid down freshwater rock slides, visited small villages that are the same now as they have been for 200 years, and went to see native dances. It was great.

After we cleared from Apia we headed for the east end of Upolu, the main island of Western Samoa. We stopped for the night at an anchorage off a village called Uafato, and were surrounded by outriggers. After a while, a small outrigger pulled up with two men on board. They told us we had to leave. It seems the local chief didn't want us in his bay.

After some discussion, and an offer to "donate" some money to the local church, (we offered $20, they wanted $50, we gave them $40), we were told we could spend the night, and that, in turn, they would bring us out some local fruits and food that evening. They showed up with one fishhead (no shit, a fishhead!), and some boiled taro root, which tastes something like unrefined book paste. It went out the starboard porthole as they were leaving via the port side.

In the morning, we were more than glad to set sail, even though the winds were right on our nose. For the next 12 hours we motorsailed into 20- to 25-knot winds, and, at dusk, pulled into Pago Pago.

The next day we waited for customs to come and clear the boat. After three hours of waiting, we decided to head over to a mooring buoy, but we were contacted by radio and instructed to pull up to the main dock. This seemed a little odd, since normally they board you at the customs dock, but we did it, and soon we were boarded by six customs officers and a flea-ridden dog. The customs people wore leather-soled brogans and stomped all over our teak, while the dog did his skidding act on the cabin sole leaving scratches and scattering fleas about the boat. The fact that they didn't find anything didn't seem to deter them. On boarding the boat, one officer said to Joel, "I guess you guys made a pretty big haul, huh?" And after they left, when they found we were clean, the same guy said, "Well, guess you got away with it this time." Sometimes you just want to play flatten-the-nose with people, but I figured customs wasn't likely to take that too well, so I let it pass. It did put a damper on the rest of the day.

A few days later Jody decided she wanted a traditional Samoan tata'u. Of course she didn't want it on her, she wanted it on me. I soon found myself having some big, old Samoan stick pins and needles in me for the next two hours. They called it a tata'u, I called it torture. But I have to admit, it does look pretty good. It's a traditional Samoan tattoo that surrounds my right ankle and depicts the sea, the islands, the fruits, fauna, and fish of Samoa. It was done at Tisa's Barefoot Bar which is a little hideaway on the beach just outside of Pago Pago. Tisa had become a good friend while we were in Samoa, and Wilson is well known not only for his Samoan tata'u style, but his tapa art work which hangs in the museum in Pago. I guess that means I'll have to ship my ankle there when I'm through with it. In any case, I ended up with a throbbing ankle and some really fine artwork on my leg. Also, I have some damn fine artwork on my back, too. No, not another tattoo. Kari designed and printed some T-shirts for the *Lost Soul Pacific Expedition* as a gift for our bringing her back from Tonga. She was a pretty well known artist, and worked with the Art Museum in Pago. The shirts looked great.

After "we" got our tata'u, we were invited by Ali and her new husband Rod to come over for a barbecue and to play around some. No, not that way! Clean up your mind! We played volleyball with a bunch of the locals.

As you know, there are good days and bad days. One day we had one of the bad ones. The night before was actually pretty good. We had dinner at Sadie's, our favorite place in Pago Pago, and turned in for a good night's sleep. At about midnight, we were hit with 30- to 35-knot winds and heavy rain. At 5 a.m., I was rudely awakened by the thump of an ugly steel boat from Germany hitting my stern. We got him pushed off and found the large, rusted, steel Navy buoy we were tied to had swung around and was rubbing against our hull. I figured this was an omen and told the crew to get ready to sail. As we cleared the island, we found the wind was blowing 25 knots. Any guesses from which direction? Of course, it was right on our nose!

We decided to make some easting as we had to go 1,200 miles to the northeast to hit Christmas Island, which is the halfway point to Hawaii. For the rest of the day we motorsailed to the east. At about 2 p.m., we saw the Manua Islands ahead. Since we had our sleep interrupted the night before, I figured we could anchor for the night at Tao Island. Of course, the sun set one hour before we got into the anchorage, and there was no moon, so we got to anchor by the Braille method.

The next morning I was amazed to find we were still afloat, had hit nothing, and the sun was shining. The water was 83 degrees and crystal clear, we did a little overboard drill and then headed out. By 10 a.m., the sun was shining, the winds had moved a little to the east, the seas were calm, and we were motorsailing again. With the Manua Islands off our stern, it was a beautiful day.

After six days beating into it we thought we'd seen enough, but each day got just a little worse. All those letters we sent to folks who were envious of where we were; well, here was their payback. I'd rather have been the night pot washer at the Blue Moon Saloon than be where I was.

When we left the Manua Islands there was no wind and we motored north. Then the wind started to blow, right on our nose, naturally, so we shifted course to head for Suvarov Island to the east. After half a day, the wind shifted onto our nose in that direction, so we changed and headed for our original destination. The wind then blew harder, up to about 25 knots, and just tight enough so we couldn't sail on the course

54

BOB BITCHIN

we wanted. A weatherfax came through and told us the wind was out of the east. We, of course, had it out of the north. Then it started to blow harder. By the next day, we had 35 knots winds and high seas, and figured it couldn't get much worse.

It got worse, 35 to 45 knots off our nose with high seas. We cut as tight as we could and made it through the day. The weatherfax said we were having a great day. Then we got the day's weather. The fax said southerly, which would blow us right to where we wanted to go. Actually, we had northerly, at 35 mph, and were making about two to three knots under power, beating into heavy seas. At night, we got a whole new experience. Just before the rains started to inundate us, we saw a lightning storm. This one was different, though. There was no thunder, and the lightning was not sheet lightning, but ball lightning. This was a whole bunch of fun. As we passed under the storm, these bright flashes looked like a spaceship using a flashbulb. It really kept our hair on end.

We had about another 600 miles to go to Christmas Island, and our steering was leaking again. We were running out of fluid. The dinghy sprung an air leak and was hanging limp off the stern. We couldn't wash dishes or make water because the boat was heeled over so far from the wind the sink overflowed from seawater and the watermaker won't work at that angle.

But we made it. For a while, we didn't think we would. It was one of those "you can't get there from here" deals. The winds blew from the northeast, the current was running over 50 miles a day westward (yeah, we were coming from the west). That meant when we were steering 60 degrees and doing seven knots motorsailing, we were actually only making three knots over the bottom. Talk about nerve wracking. I thought I'd never get to Christmas Island, but after some fancy tacking and two extra days at sea, we made it.

All of a sudden we were anchored off a beautiful white sand beach with the only two other boats there, a 35 footer from Maui, and a 500-foot U.S. Navy vessel. Just what we needed, 350 Navy guys. Jody was in heaven.

The guys were buzzing the boat whenever she went topside in a bathing suit. Of course, there were some limp-wristed guys who came by singing show tunes whenever Luke or Joel went on deck, too. Guess Clinton got the boys a place to serve, huh?

Kiritimati (somehow they pronounce that Christmas, as the "ti" is pronounced "ts") was a real oddity for our travels. It was used to make people glow in the sixties (A-bomb tests) and the place looked like it was wiped out. Rusted hulks everywhere, and rubble wherever you'd look. But the atoll was beautiful and the lagoon had about 200 shades of blue and green. Anyway, after turning the island radioactive in the sixties, they decided it was okay to live there again, so they moved a bunch of folks from the Gilbert Islands, who are now the residents. They were very friendly and, no, they don't glow at night.

The next day we got to haul fuel to the boat. That means we got four 55-gallon drums delivered to the beach, and then we got to siphon the fuel into five-gallon jugs and take 'em, by dinghy, to the boat. What fun!

The LOST SOUL Is Saved

>————◄————

Y ou won't believe this one! The Catholic priest for the
Line Islands and Kiribati, Father Gracien Bermond,
has asked the LOST SOUL for a ride to the next island, Fanning,
which is about 160 miles from here. Check it out, a priest on
the LOST SOUL. I think he may find this to be his most difficult
saving job. We told the crew to hide their *Hustler* and *Pent-
house* magazines. Then all we had to do was see if we could
get through two days without swearing.

We had a great sail to Fanning. We even got to run our
spinnaker and mizzen staysail. Once inside the lagoon at Fanning, we found friendly people and a gorgeous island, somewhat reminiscent of the Tuamotu atolls. Since there hadn't
been a supply boat to come through in over a year, the people
were real happy to get the supplies we'd brought in. Father
Bermond asked for a ride to Washington Island, which is
about 80 miles from there, and after he described it to us,
well, we had to go there. We had no charts for it, but the father
swore (well, not really swore, but you know what I mean) that
it was there, and that there are even people on it. Sunday, after
his last service, we hoisted anchor and did an overnighter to
Washington Island.

But first we explored Fanning, and it is one of the prettiest stops we'd made yet. The lagoon is a brilliant blue/green,
and the motus that surround it have the softest white sand
we've seen this trip. At Fanning there has never been a cy-
clone or hurricane because it's only a couple degrees off the
equator.

Talk about an idyllic lifestyle. We spent three days exploring motus and skinny-dipping on deserted white sand

beaches. Even in the middle of the lagoon, there are coral reefs covered with sand that you can stop on, with the water up to your knees, but a mile from land.

When you're cruising you tend to forget that the people you visit may not be as, shall we say, "traveled." This was shown to us one afternoon by Father Bermond. Earlier in the day he'd suggested we might trade some food for gas for our dinghy. We were running low, and they had a 55-gallon drum, full. It seems that the Australian government had given Fanning Island a Land Rover for their use. The fact that there were no roads, nor is any motu longer than 100 yards didn't seem to faze them.

So, anyway, they have this Land Rover, and a 55-gallon drum of fuel is delivered every year. Having no use for it, they said they'd be glad to trade for some food, since they had no stores on the island, and hadn't seen a freighter in over a year.

We went back to the boat and packed up a little care package for them. We threw in a couple of cans of fresh fruit, vegetables, some Spam, and, as a last thought, a two-kilo brick of New Zealand white cheddar cheese, kind of a *pièce de résistance*.

When we went ashore the matai of the village met us at the small palapa platform by the beach. We opened our bag and set the cans of fruit down, and his eyes brightened. When he saw the vegetables he actually started to grin. But when he saw the Spam he couldn't control himself, and broke into a full-fledged smile. It seems that Spam is like roast beef on Fanning.

When I took out the cheddar I expected him to start giggling, but it had just the opposite effect. He just kind of looked at it, shrugged his shoulders, and led us to the gasoline.

About two hours later Father Bermond comes and he is laughing out loud as his small boat pulls alongside the LOST SOUL.

"What's so funny?" I asked.

"Bob," he said, "have you ever seen any cows on this island?"

I thought a moment.

"No, I don't guess I have." I stammered. "Why do you ask?"

"Well," he smiled, "what made you think these people would know what cheese was? The people waited until you left, went back to the palapa, and cut into your gift. When the odor of the cheddar came wafting out they thought whatever it was you gave them was bad, and they fed it to the pigs!"

He laughed a little, and then went on.

"It almost broke my heart. Do you have any idea how long it's been since I've had any cheese?" he hesitated a second. "After all, I am a Frenchman!"

That night we fed him macaroni and cheese for dinner, with a couple of large wedges of New Zealand cheddar.

We gave Father Bermond a ride to Washington Island. Even though we didn't have any charts of the island itself, it was on our way to Palmyra. We left him at Washington Island without dropping anchor. It seems the good father forgot to tell us one thing. You can't anchor there. It is a beautiful island, just like he said. It has giant banyan trees, brilliant, white sand beaches, and deep jungle foliage, but there is no place that is protected to drop an anchor and no place to land a dinghy. Five men came out to meet us as we approached at dawn and took the good father off our hands. As I watched them beach their boat I gave thanks that it was them and not us. They just wait between six-foot setting waves and go full speed at the beach. I still haven't figured out how they get the boat back off the beach.

The good news is Palmyra Island. We have saved the best for last. Palmyra is like an atoll but it has three lagoons. It was used as a base in the Second World War, and over 6,000 people lived there, but the jungle has taken it back, and now there is just one man, a Frenchman named Roger, who lives there as a caretaker. There are wrecked planes, bunkers, and other war relics covered with jungle vegetation, and a million birds. A billion fish fill the lagoons, and the fishing and diving is phenomenal. It is only five degrees off the equator, so it's out of the hurricane zone and the strongest winds they get here are 25 to 30 knots. It is just 900 miles south of Hawaii, and it has an airfield that could land 747s, if you could get the birds off it. There is a lagoon that can take up to 300-foot vessels with 22 feet bottom clearance through the pass and over 100-foot depth in the lagoon.

We put off our intended departure date because we loved the place so much. It's like a cross between Fantasy Island and Gilligan's Island.

Excitement! Excitement!

➤◀

*T*hey say that sailing is 90 percent boredom and 10 percent sheer panic. Well, the next couple of days were the sheer panic part. A slow boat to Palmyra, and a 170-ton fishing boat on the reef, all in two days. Three days prior we got a radio call from a 65-foot ferrocement sailboat, the HEATHER MARIA, saying they were 28 miles out and were trying to get in by dark. At sunset, they arrived, so we had our crewman Joel take Roger out to guide them in with our dinghy, since all he had was a sailing dinghy. By the time they hit the pass, it was too late, but we had three squalls come through while the boys were out there looking for them, and they almost blew out of sight of the island, without a compass to find their way back in. The next day, HEATHER MARIA had blown 17 miles out to sea, and it took her 10 hours to get back that far. The seas were up and squalls kept blowing through but finally, at sunset, they were guided into the lagoon to the cheers of their Kiwi, African, French, and Canadian crew.

The next evening, we were sitting on our poop deck enjoying the sunset with Pete, off the boat ENDORA, and John and Tasha, of WIND-I-GO, when we saw a fishing boat approaching the island. Roger reached them on the radio and they said they had been into the lagoon before and could make it in easily.

A few minutes later, they were awash on the reef, just a few hundred feet from a couple of old hulks that went aground in the past. The boat was MAVERICK, a 170-ton fishing boat on its way from Honolulu to Pago Pago with 70 tons of albacore. It was not insured and cost over a million dollars. The owner, Mike, his wife and their infant daughter were aboard.

•••

During the night, they tried to get off, and were washed farther and farther onto the reef. By dawn, they were almost a quarter of a mile into the "Potato Patch," a patch of coral heads that were only three or four feet deep, and MAVERICK drew ten feet!

All morning, Roger, Pete, John, and I helped Mike lay cable and rope trying to pull her off with the hydraulic winch. Then the tide went down and she was sitting on the bottom, hard. Everybody took a couple of hours to get some sleep, and at 2:30 in the afternoon, when the tide started rising, we were back at it. Slowly, a few feet at a time, with Mike in the water all day, attaching cable and rope to the base of coral heads, the rest of us hauled in on it and just before sunset we were only a few meters from the channel. Mike jumped into the pilothouse and fired up the engines. I stood by with a knife to cut the rope that was holding us in place, while Roger and Pete got in the dinghy to pull the rope away from the props as we cut it. At a signal, I cut the rope and the dinghy pulled it away, Mike hit the throttles and the engines roared into action, pushing the 170 tons through water and small coral heads, and free into the deep.

That night, Mike and his wife made a dinner for us we couldn't believe. Steak, potatoes, fresh fruit, salad, dessert, and ice-cold beer, which we hadn't seen any since Pago Pago, and lots of Jack Daniels. It was a great party. In just two days, some long-time, fast friendships were made in a struggle to do what looked impossible.

We left Palmyra Island for Hawaii, about a 1,000-mile sail. We'd been out of touch for a few months, and needed to check in. The first day was great. At about 10 p.m. Luke was on watch, when all of sudden the boat spun around like Jack Benny hearing a coin drop, and all control was lost. I jumped down the companionway and ran back to the steering post under the aft cabin bunk. There, I found the gudgeon that held the rudder was as shattered as last year's resolutions. We had no rudder. Now, if I were to have a list as to what I could do without, the rudder would be the last item on it. Without a rudder, you cannot steer the ship. If you can't steer the ship, you go around in little circles, and if you go around in little circles you don't get anywhere. We were 55 miles out from Palmyra, and about eyeball-deep in doodoo. We dropped our sails, and started to rig a Mickey Mouse steering system. We had an emergency tiller stored belowdeck, so we broke it out. I grabbed the handle that was bolted in place and pushed it to starboard.

It broke off in my hand. Just what we didn't need, a rusted emergency tiller, with a broken shaft. After checking it out for a couple of minutes, I figured a way to fix it, and we set to work. We attached a long pole to the rudder post, and two pipe wrenches on that. We faced the two wrenches toward each other and tied them tight with a small piece of rope. This gave us a tiller of sorts. We had to push the pipe wrench with our legs, with all our strength, to steer the 42-ton boat. I put out a Pan-Pan (emergency) message on the radio, and we started to try to steer back to Palmyra. About 35 miles out we were heard by MAVERICK, the boat we helped haul off the reef two days earlier. In a while, he had contacted the other three boats at the island, and they took shifts monitoring the radio to see if we were going to make it in. For 10 hours we steered by sheer leg power, with Joel and Luke sitting in for most of that time. Without them as crew, I don't know if we'd have made it. Nothing like four 19-year-old legs to get you through. By dawn, the crew of the LOST SOUL, with eyes as red as Tammy Faye's lips, were met in the channel and guided in to anchor in Palmyra.

Then the unbelievable happened. Mike, the captain of

MAVERICK, said he had a complete metal shop on board. Pete, on ELSBEN, was a millwright and a metal engineer, and John, on WIND-I-GO, had spent the last 35 years building boats in Australia, New Zealand, and Hawaii. The three of them met me on the boat and removed the shattered part while I walked around in a daze. I was sure it could never be repaired. While we caught a couple of hours of much-needed sleep, they welded, re-designed, and re-built my steering gudgeon. When I awoke at noon, they came aboard and installed an almost-new part. This is something that I would have had a hard time doing in a city like Honolulu in a week, and they did it on a deserted island in the middle of the South Pacific in a few hours. Unbelievable.

If I never believed in karma before, I do now. Two days earlier, I had helped save a man's boat, and because of that, two days later, he saves mine.

That night, the four boats anchored at this isolated island in the middle of the Pacific had a little party. A potluck dinner on shore. There is no describing the feeling of sitting around a fire with these people who literally saved our lives. Life doesn't get any better than this.

In the morning, we pulled alongside MAVERICK and took on some fuel he gave us to top our tanks and, once again, we were off for Hawaii.

The day we left Palmyra we were all in great spirits. Full tanks, a fixed steering head, and a great trip to Hawaii ahead of us. The winds were even in our favor.

Two hours later our mainsail ripped, so we reefed it below the tear point. Then, the worst happened. The transmission took a poop. It just stopped working. All of a sudden, we were without a transmission and in the doldrums.

For two days we'd been trying to maintain a speed of

three knots, but one night we sat becalmed for hours. I got so depressed about sitting still that I fired the engine, and after exhausting every way I could think of to jury-rig it to work, I just put it into reverse and tried to back to Hawaii. That was so funny we all started to laugh, and our sanity was saved for the moment. It was raining for those two days. Then we had a weatherfax that said we'd have a tropical depression just 200 miles east of us, and it was headed our way.

'Tis times like these that try men's (lost) souls. After two days of alternating storms and dead calms, we were into the third straight day of no wind. Just the flopping of sails and the breaking of stuff. In the night, we did a half dozen donuts. No, not the kind you eat, the kind your boat does when there is ab-solutely no wind. You go in circles, trying to find wind. We made almost 37 miles in a full day. That's a neck-breaking one-and-a-half knots, or about half the speed you can walk. Imagine walking 950 miles from Palmyra to Hawaii. Yeah, that's how we felt, too. The ice maker broke loose with the swaying and banged into the propane switch, breaking it. Then the light switch broke off. The fuse in the battery charger blew six times, we had two fuses left, and our electri-cal system said we had reversed polarity. We couldn't get the single sideband radio to work. Put this all together with the transmission being out, so we just had to sit there, and you had a real Xanax kind of day.

Until the morning. At dawn, I figured sitting and snivel-ing was about as good as sending money to the Reverend Jimmy Baker, so I got to work. I ripped out the ice maker and built a new shelf for it, found the short that caused the battery charger to reverse polarity and fixed that, fixed the propane switch, and figured I had a start on the day.

That was, until we went on deck. There we found three new holes in the sail (# 12, 13 and 14), a batten slide torn loose and a reef line worn through. Hard to believe this was a new sail. After we fixed that, we found that the starboard headsail sheet was holding by a thread. We had to lower the headsail and make a new sheet line for it.

By then it was 9:30 a.m. All was well with the world, but we were still sitting and waiting for a puff of breeze. In the doldrums of the equator, with no wind, and without a motor, there is no motion. Take my word for it.

Aloha

━━━━━━━━━━━━━━◄►━━━━━━━━━━━━━━

*A*t dawn, after ten days at sea without an engine, Luke and I spotted Mauna Kea and Mauna Loa, the two peaks on the big island of Hawaii. It was most heartening. Now, all we had to do was go the 164 miles to Ala Wai Harbor on Oahu and we would be ready to start fixing all the things we'd broken on the boat in the previous 11,000 miles and nine months. I could see my bank account dwindling faster than Pee Wee Herman's reputation.

But it did feel pretty good, and, don't tell the crew, but I was damn proud of 'em. A thousand miles across the Pacific, including the equator, without an engine, is quite a fea., and in 10 days it's almost a miracle. Of course, I told them it was normal.

Okay, so maybe civilization isn't so bad. We had been sitting there in front of the Hawaii Yacht Club in the Ala Wai Marina near Waikiki for almost two weeks. About 50 feet from our boat was the yacht club bar, where the drinks were good and very inexpensive.

After we fixed all that miscellaneous and sundry broken stuff and spent all the money we had, we decided we needed to go to some other islands and sail off for a few weeks.

We headed across the channel to Lahaina, where we stayed for the next three days. Lahaina, on the island of Maui, is an old whaling village that has kept its atmosphere, and in doing so, has attracted more tourists than any other Hawaiian city except Waikiki. There were so many tourists there was a constant oil slick on the beach from their suntan lotions.

After five days in Lahaina, and after driving our rent-a-wreck on every road that was marked "do not drive a rent-a-car here," it was time to leave again. There was going to be a Thanksgiving dinner at the Hawaii Yacht Club, and I love to eat. We had to get there.

We waited until morning, and took off into the Molokai Channel.

As we set across the channel, the winds were blowing at 35 knots. By mid-channel they were up to 45 knots, and the waves were running from 18 to 22 feet high. No, that's not my estimate, that is what the weather radio said. I think they were closer to 30 feet. One of the fool things was so big that it broke over the whole boat. Talk about wet! Of course, we were ready for it. When we set out, it was with no mizzen, a double-reefed main, no fore staysail, and a storm jib. Actually, it wasn't too bad, and it was exciting seeing seas that big. Besides that, we got a lot of respect when we pulled in at the Hawaii Yacht Club. They couldn't believe we braved those seas just to get there for Thanksgiving. I guess they didn't know how much we like turkey and stuffing!

Anyway, we made the crossing from hell, and were tucked in beautiful Waikiki, and, once again, were being spoiled rotten. I can't recommend decadence as a way of life, but it was working for me.

Joel flew home to Canada and Luke would soon be flying to the land of great white-outs. They had been out for a year and were going back to college and to work. We knew we'd miss 'em.

But we had some new crew. Just in case you guys weren't jealous enough, I would be breaking in two new crew members while cruising the islands. Two cute, little, blonde hard-bodies with sailing experience. Just imagine, alone at sea for months with three pretty young ladies. At my age, it could be dangerous, but I wasn't scared. I knew it was going to be tough when I sailed off into the sunset, and I had to live with the cards I was given. I would endeavor to persevere.

Island Exploring

————————◄————————

*F*or the past three days I had been sailing between some of the nicest islands in the North Pacific, with the best crew I could imagine. Not only was the new crew efficient, they were also damn good to look at. The hardest part about being the only man on board was keeping my mind on sailing.

It was April, and April is a good month to cruise the Hawaiian Islands. After our 15,000 mile trek to and through the South Pacific, the sailing in the North Pacific seemed a little more, uh, shall we say, aggressive?

That's the word all right. It seems that whenever we sailed anywhere in the Hawaiian Islands, the winds were either blowing up a gale, or a bit stronger, and they always came out of the direction you were going.

All of that aside, after undergoing enough repairs to make Bill Gates flinch, the LOST SOUL was ready to do a little island exploring.

Our crew for this voyage consisted of two beautiful, displaced blonde ski bunnies, Janet and Samantha, from Colorado, one lovely first mate, Jody, and of course one not too bright but eager, tattooed captain.

I swear there were tears in the eyes of the male membership at the Hawaii Yacht Club as my crew cast off the lines for our departure. Not because the LOST SOUL was leaving. No, rather it was due to the crew leaving. Their working attire of choice consisted of black, string bikinis. Well, it's hot in Hawaii! The bar at the yacht club did an excellent business on the days the girls would sand and varnish, or wash the boat. The members constantly sent drinks down to them from the bar.

•-•

The winds blew down hard during our first cruise through the islands. Even though I'd sailed Hawaii three or four times previously, this time the winds seemed to blow just a little harder, a little longer, and from more directions.

Our sail to Lahaina was directly into the wind, and consisted of three stops along the way, one night on Molokai, one night on Lanai, and then into Lahaina, Maui.

Once there, it was real rough due to a kona storm coming out of the south. We tied up to a mooring buoy belonging to the Lahaina Yacht Club. In the morning I dove overboard and tied an extra line to the buoy as insurance. Good thing—for the next 10 days we had rain, winds, and nasties.

My brother, Dr. Al, the kiddies' pal, flew in, and the next day we sailed to the atoll of Molokini to do some diving. This is the tip of a volcano that sticks up about 80 feet out of the water and is in a "C" shape about 600 feet in diameter.

It has been set aside as a reserve for sea life, and is excellent for diving. We had to find a mooring to tie to. There is no anchoring. In the morning it fills with tour boats, so we found it best to pull in during the afternoon, and dive early, leaving when the tourists arrived.

Next we were off to Kona on the big island of Hawaii. This trip turned out to be the most fun of all.

While we sat waiting for better winds, we spotted some whales, and the next thing we knew we were bouncing along in our Zodiac after three large humpbacks that were playing near the rocky shore. We followed them for awhile and it was great. They kept coming to the surface and checking us out as we checked them out.

We snorkeled off the white sand beach of Ahihi Bay, and generally had a great time. Samantha, Janet, and Jody got tans while Al and I just lazed about wondering what our friends back home would have to say about all this.

On our crossing from Maui to the Big Island of Hawaii, we had the best weather we'd seen in Hawaii. We awoke at five a.m. and headed out. By six the sun was coming up over the Big Island while the full moon was setting over Kahoolawe. The island of Hawaii is made up of two large mountains - Mauna Loa and Mauna Kea. Mauna Loa is actually the highest mountain in the world, if you count the part that is underwater. It rises over 30,000 feet from the ocean floor, and over 13,000 feet above sea level.

As we crossed, the clouds burned off, and for the first time in over 12 years of cruising the Hawaiian waters I saw the tops of both mountains, and both of them were snow-capped! Since Janet and Samantha are both avid skiers from Aspen, they couldn't wait to write their friends and tell 'em we had more snowfall in Hawaii than they had in Aspen.

After a few days in Kailua, we sailed south to Kealakekua. This is where Captain Cook, the man who discovered the Hawaiian Islands and more than half the Pacific, was killed. It's a marine reserve now. At night we were the only boat in the bay, and it was phenomenal. In the mornings we were surrounded by fish so plentiful they looked like they were solid enough to walk across. We threw them handfuls of granola and they frenzied. We had a lot of fun swimming among them. In fact, the diving in Kealakekua was better than any we had seen in our trip through the South Pacific. There were more fish there, of more varieties than we believed possible.

While diving, we found a bronze plaque in the water that marked the exact spot where Captain Cook was killed. An additional monument on shore was surrounded by several plaques placed there over the past 100 years commemorating his discoveries, like Samoa, Tonga, Australia, and, of course the Cook Islands.

It was also a surprise to find out that while he was here in Hawaii his cartographer who drew the first charts was Lieutenant William Bligh. He later became the famous Captain Bligh, of the ship BOUNTY.

A few days later, we sailed to Waikoloa on the northwest part of Hawaii. We sailed there to see Jeff Kalback whom we'd met on Christmas Island. He was running the catamaran SEA SMOKE, a whale watch boat out of the Royal Waikoloa Hotel. The original owner of the boat was James Arness from the TV series *Gunsmoke*, and it held the world speed record for sailboats back in the sixties, doing over 30 knots. It sailed to Hawaii in less than nine days, also setting a record back then.

We were given a mooring to use in the harbor and spent the next few days visiting with friends.

One day Captain Jeff invited us to come along on SEA SMOKE for a sunset cruise. We waited in the bar by the pool until it was time to load up, and then we boarded. After we were out of the channel Jeff asked if I wanted to take the wheel for awhile as he went forward to schmooze with the paying guests. I jumped at the chance, and was soon steering a lazy course up the coast of Hawaii. Jody came up and brought me a cold beer, and I chugged it down, enjoying the cool liquid in the heat of the afternoon.

Then one of the guests came up to me.

"Weren't you in the bar having a beer just before we took off?" he asked.

"Why yes, I was." I smiled back at him.

"And you're having a beer now, while you run the boat?" he asked, a little incredulously.

I looked at the cool brew in my hand, and turned it up, to down the last few drops. "Yup," I said, "it tastes damn good, too."

"Well," he huffed, "as a licensed Captain I'd think you

would know better than to drink while you handle a boat full of people."

I thought for a second, gave him my biggest white-toothed grin, and said, "Yeah, yer probably right," I said, " but I don't have a license, so it's no problem."

He looked a little shocked, and went back to his seat. Jeff came over and took the wheel, and we had a great laugh.

Then it was time to sail to Maui so my brother could fly back to the mainland. The folks on SEA SMOKE decided we needed some guidance to get across the Alenuihaha Channel. Also, they needed some fun sailing, and a day off. So Jeff McConnel (we call him McJeff) and Jeff Kalback (our old friend from Christmas Island) and Carolyn (a new friend we'd met there in Waikoloa) were added to our crew list. In the morning, the eight of us took off for the big crossing. With our crew of three captains, a Ph.D., and four fine looking women, we were set for anything.

Actually, this trip turned out to be, once again, one of the best crossings we made. When it blows 20 knots elsewhere, it will blow 40 knots in the Alenui. By mid-morning, we started to hit the winds and we really were flying. Before we finished the crossing we had hit a boat speed of 13 knots three times (okay, so we were surfing when it happened!), once under each captain's hand, and averaged over 10 knots for the 59-mile crossing. That's fast on a 42-ton boat. We did this with a single reefed mainsail and a reefed headsail. No mizzen, no fore-staysail. Just two reefed sails. It was fantastic.

When we arrived at McKenna Beach on Maui we set our anchor and soon saw a group of whales swimming near us. That night three whales surrounded our boat. At two a.m. they swam within 15 feet of us. There was a small calf, the mother, and an escort. You could hear them talking through the hull of the boat and no one aboard slept as they swam around us, investigating.

In the morning, we took Jeff, McJeff, and Carolyn ashore. The landing was pretty funny. Here we had three licensed captains and we still couldn't land a 13-foot boat on shore without everyone getting wet. They were picked up by a friend and flew back to the Big Island of Hawaii on a private plane, wet clothes and all. We hoisted anchor and sailed on to Lahaina.

My brother had to fly home, so we hung out there in Lahaina until his flight. I really hated to see him go. We'd spent more time together on this trip than we had in the past 35 years, since he'd gone off to join the Marines.

While in Maui, we ran into a woodcarver by the name of Joe, who conned us into having him carve a lifesized dolphin for a figure head on the LOST SOUL. When he finished, we dashed back to Ala Wai Harbor to mount her on the bow. The new mascot of the boat was carved from monkeypod wood. Her name was Dolly Wood Dolphin, but we just called her Dolly Wood. She was very cool, and added a lot of class to the boat.

After a quick flight home for my fiftieth birthday party, it was time to go out and do some sailing again.

As luck would have it, the morning we were to leave, the highest winds in years hit the islands. Seventy knot winds and 35-foot seas in the channels. We came down with a case of sanity and opted to sit for the next five days at the Hawaii Yacht Club waiting for the winds to settle.

The day came when the weatherman said it was okay to hit the high seas, so Jody and I dropped the dock lines and headed out for a few weeks of solitary sailing. Samantha and Janet had flown back to Aspen as the season was starting, and we were left to our own devices.

As we came around Diamond Head, we were hit with 30 knots of wind on our nose. We set a double reef and small yankee and we motorsailed to the end of Oahu. At Koko Head, we were hit with winds up to 35 knots, and now the seas were running 12 to 18 feet. "What the hell," we said, "let's go for it!"

Seven hours later, we pulled into Lono Harbor on Molokai after what was the wettest crossing I can recall. It blew stink all the way.

In the morning, it was still blowing, but it was only about 25 miles across the channel to Five Needles on the island of Lanai. We double reefed the main again, and headed out into it. After all, how bad could it be? The weatherman assured us the bad weather was over, right?

About a half hour out we were fighting 45- to 50-knot winds 25 degrees off our bow, with 22- to 25-foot seas breaking over us. The 22 miles from Lono to the lee of Lanai was the roughest sail I can recall, even rougher than the day before. We finally got behind some cliffs and found a place to anchor, where we sat for two days, waiting for some "good" weather.

After a couple of days watching Star Wars videos, we opted to go out into it and find a better place to sit. We motored around Lanai and found ourselves in the lee of Mount Haleakala on Maui, the third highest mountain in Hawaii. We motored to Ahihi on the east end of Maui and spent the night in relative comfort.

I say relative because at three a.m. the winds switched to the north-northeast and we found ourselves riding the high seas again. The weather radio said there was a high wind advisory, but it would be out of the northeast. For the past three weeks the winds had been howling out of the east. The next day the wind would drop to under 45 knots, but out of the east again, on our nose as we crossed the Alenuihaha.

Being dumber than dirt (I showed my intelligence when I bought the boat in the first place!), I decided to head out and cross the channel while there was a high wind warning, because it was almost in the right direction, rather than wait for it to switch onto our nose, and lessen.

Fifty-two miles later, Jody and I dropped to our knees and thanked all the gods that be for our lives. In 28 years of sailing, this took the cake. I'd seen hurricanes and gales, but the Alenuihaha Channel, in full gale, tops everything.

The seas were mountainous. We figure they were about 28 to 30 feet. That meant the wave faces were almost 60 feet high. The winds were coming out of the northeast, but they were coming at 50-55 miles. Waves broke over the boat so many times we thought we were in a saltwater washing machine.

The Thrill of a Lifetime

T he ultimate thrill was when we had a rogue wave hit. All of a sudden Jody's eyes were very round. Just as I was about to ask her why, the boat stopped heeling and sat bolt-upright. "That's odd," I thought, "with over 50 knots of wind, you'd think we'd stay heeled." I looked back over my shoulder, and wished I hadn't. The reason for Jody's cow-eyes was self-evident. We were about to be slammed by an 80-foot breaking wave.

Maybe I wasn't quite that blasé about it. In fact, as I think back on it, I was actually in a state of shock. We were down in the valley of this huge mamuu of a wave, looking up almost 100 feet to its clear crest.

Clear? That could only mean one thing. The damn thing's about to break! All over us!

The LOST SOUL didn't seem to really care one way or the other. Her 42 tons started to raise as the wave began to slide under her. We were heading slightly down swell, because we'd been trying to cut the seas as best we could. As we went up the face of this humongous wave the boat started to heel to starboard, as the port side was higher on the wave. The elevator ride up was smooth . . . until the sail popped out from behind the wave, and was hit full-on by the 50- to 55-knot winds. That caused the boat to heel to a sickening angle, almost 90 degrees, as there was little to no water under the starboard side of the boat.

Then the wave broke.

I hooked my arm through the steering wheel, and Jody held tight to the handrail above her head. It all was happening in slow motion. The boat went from upright to 90 degrees, and then the breaking wave knocked us over until the mast was actually pointing down, into the sea.

We'd been doing about eight knots under a triple reefed main and handkerchief of a headsail, and all of a sudden the forward motion stopped as the sail went under. The wave broke completely and the water went right over us. I noticed the boat was trying to right itself. Then the 30,000 pounds of keel took hold, and was lifting the mast and sails out of the sea; we were righted, and back on course. It looked like a giant waterfall as hundreds of thousands of gallons of water poured from the cup of the sail. It was beautiful. The sun sparkled on every bit of the wet boat, and before I even knew it we were starting to pull in the same direction we were going when we were hit.

I looked back over my shoulder at the peak of Haleakala on Maui. In front of us, in the crisp and clear windblown distance I could see the snowcapped peaks of Mauna Kea and Mauna Loa. We were slamming our way there and enjoying every second. Talk about excitement! It's times like this that let you know you are alive. You can feel the vibrations and it wells up inside of you.

It was at about this time in my life when I fully appreciated the saying, "When it comes to rigging, there is no such thing as overkill." Because we had 14 oversized stays per mast, we were not dismasted.

It was a blast! Jody and I had to steer the boat the rest of the way across as our autopilot took the day off after that, and the excitement was maximum all the way. We didn't hit calm water until we passed our friend Jeff on SEA SMOKE, about ½ mile out of Waikoloa, as he was taking out a sunset cruise in the lee of the island. We picked up a mooring there and settled in at the bar at the Royal Waikoloa Hotel.

The winds started to die the next day, and the sun came out for the first time in weeks. All the bad weather and hellacious seas were behind us, and once again we felt like we might be doing the right thing living on a boat in Hawaii.

For the next week we were to experience the best weather we'd had the entire trip. Each day was perfect. Soft breezes, warm sunshine and calm seas. We just lazed about, and went out on SEA SMOKE a few times.

When the week was up, we really hated to drop the mooring and head out, but we had a new crew flying into Honolulu for the sail back to the mainland, so we had to get back to Oahu.

Jeff K. got a couple of days off and volunteered to help us sail back across the Alenuihaha Channel. The winds were reported to be down to gentle trades, and it looked as if it would be a good crossing.

And it was. We had 25-knot winds off our stern and cruised at 9 to 10 knots with an occasional 11 and one time even 12 knots! We went straight into Lahaina and as we approached under full sail the radio started to call us. It seems everyone there remembered us from our previous stays. Everyone wanted to know where we'd be that night. There were over a dozen people waiting for us when we hit Lahaina coolers that night, and even a couple of folks from the Hawaii Yacht Club who'd seen us sail in. It was a great party. Of course, there were a few folks disappointed that our crew was no longer with us.

A few days later, Skip and the rest of our new crew arrived, Dan "the Slug Man", a marine biologist who collects sea slugs and owns a Hudson 46 ketch, flew in for the voyage. Also, Andrew, who owns a Vagabond 47 ketch, and who soon earned the nickname "Squid" flew in. So our crew was set, Skip, Squid, and the Slug Man along with Jody and myself.

We took a day to stock the boat, and then we were off. We left at sunset for a night sail to Kauai. No one slept that night due to the excitement of leaving on our Pacific crossing.

Sightseeing on a Schedule

*T*he following day we paid dearly. Even though we had no sleep, we decided we needed to do a little sightseeing before the long trek to the mainland. We rented a big old gas-guzzling, purple Lincoln Town Car, piled the troops inside, and did a one-day whirlwind tour of Kauai. We drove up the winding road to Waimea Canyon. I don't think the crew liked my Mario Andretti driving style and, as soon as their knuckles were back to a normal color, we toured the north shore including a real neat swim in an underground fresh water cave.

The crew spent one-third of the time sleeping in their seats, one-third guzzling espresso trying to stay awake to see the sights. The final third was spent in stark terror of the 6'4" tattooed crazy man driving the purple Lincoln. That night we slept the sleep of the dead.

At dawn on April 16 we set off for the 2,700-mile eastward trek across the Pacific. The first four days we fought our way due north into 20- to 25-knot winds and moderate, 8- to 10-foot seas, all right on our nose. I was trying a new route, to only go north far enough to hit the center of the Pacific High. I planned to motor through it and head straight to the mainland instead of going north of it to the roaring 40s. On the fourth day, we got a break and the winds started to move around a little so we could make a little easting along with the northing, but it was still a long way to go.

As it turned out, my new route worked better than expected. On the morning of the fifth day out of Hawaii, one of the two boats who'd left Hawaii in front of us, CINNAMON, came on the high seas radio with some bad news. They'd been hit by a freak wave during a gale and were dismasted, at almost the halfway point, some 1,500 miles from San Francisco and 1,200 miles from Hawaii. The good news was, their engine was good and they were going to try and motor across. The bad news was they would be short by about 100 gallons of fuel. For the next few hours we transferred information to the Coast Guard for them on the single sideband radio, and then it was just waiting to see what could be done for what seemed like forever. We were still 650 miles behind them, and were trying to get there to give them what fuel we had to help them out. That evening, the Coast Guard found a freighter that would be transiting the area and had some fuel. They scheduled to meet at mid-sea for a transfer.

While all this excitement was going on, we came to the Pacific High. It was lower than expected and we first started to encounter the moderating winds.

More fun and excitement on the LOST SOUL. First of all, while sailing as tight as we could into the wind to get north, we managed to do a couple of donuts. Dan held the record for awhile, but then I caught him with two apiece. It seems that when you hit a couple of 12- to 15-foot swells you stop dead. Then, if the wind whips a little across your bow you do a big circle.

This wouldn't be too bad, except it wrapped our fishing line around our prop, so Dan the Slug Man got to do a little dive and cut at about 27 degrees latitude freeing our prop.

Awhile later, we met the true *lost soul*. It was a Hawaiian spotted owl lost at sea. We saw him winging his way towards us about 500 miles from land, with three albatross hot on his trail. To say he was exhausted would be an understatement. He landed on our dinghy and ignored us as we tried to feed him salmon, lettuce, and oranges. All he wanted to do was sleep, and sleep he did, for the next 10 hours. We named him "Dinghy" (due to his choice of landing sites) and Jody had tears in her eyes when Dinghy decided to leave us at about 10:30 that night.

A couple days later, one week after leaving Hawaii, we reached the Pacific High's center. This is a point that most people sailing from Hawaii to the mainland have to head over to get into the westerly winds. We hit it at 29 degrees, we turned on a heading towards home and started the long trek across the remaining 1,770 miles. By early morning the winds were off our stern and we popped our 2,500 square foot spinnaker. Then we added the 1,500 foot mizzen staysail and we were sailing at eight knots downwind under 4,000 feet of sail—unheard of at this point in the Pacific.

In the early afternoon, our dream sail ended abruptly as we heard a loud pop and saw our spinnaker separate from the boat at the tack. We scrambled to get it under control and on board. Once on board, we found that the tack line, a ½-inch steel cable, had separated. No big deal, and we decided we could jury-rig a new line when we needed it. That evening we entered a fog bank which limited our visibility to about 100 yards. It lasted until dawn.

For the next week, we played tag with the Pacific High. As we motored northeast and then eastward we started to think we'd never get out of it. As we moved, it moved. At one point the weatherfax showed it to be over 2,400 miles across from east to west. As the days rolled by so did the High. A week later, we were still in it with no sign of popping out the eastern end. We started to think the big "H" we saw on the weatherfax was in reality painted on top of our boat.

A little weather note here. The winds around the Pacific High rotate in a clockwise motion. We needed to get out of the High to catch the northerlies so we could sail down into California. Our fuel range is limited to about 1,500 miles, and the crossing is a little over 2,700 miles in all.

The plan was to motorsail through the heart of the High. It saves a lot of cold weather. Unfortunately, the High kept moving to the east. The farther we sailed, the High just kept moving with us. Instead of being in the High for two or three days, as we planned, we just stayed in the High as it moved east.

The sailing was unreal. No high winds, no high waves, no big seas, just a calm flat sea with either no wind at all or 10 to 15 knots of breeze, which moved us along at about seven knots. Passing through the High was the calmest sailing I'd seen in seven Pacific crossings. For days, we'd leave the sails untouched and the autopilot on as we drifted through the Pacific.

Of course, all good things must come to an end, but for a full two weeks we enjoyed a crossing most cruisers would envy. Dan had a birthday as we were in mid-Pacific and Jody outdid herself by making homemade sourdough rolls, a London broil, vegetables, mashed potatoes and gravy, and of course a birthday cake complete with 43 candles (almost burned down the boat with that much flame). We sailed with the winds off our aft port side, with calm seas and making about 150 miles a day, without a doubt the best part of the crossing. Just day after day of sunshine, good breezes and everything on the boat working fine.

As we approached the California coast we got our first real winds of the crossing. Passing Point Conception we had about 25 knots, but that was it.

It was then we realized that we didn't have a chart of Catalina Island, where we planned on making our landfall. It was here we had our going away party, and it seemed right we returned to the same spot.

At two a.m. we approached the west end light, and, using

Sunset on the equator on our first crossing to the South Pacific

Nuku Hiva. Our first stop in the South Pacific

The crew in Bora Bora
(Left to right) Jill Albro, Bob, Jody, Curt Albro

Sunset over Bora-Bora taken from a small
atoll on the outskirts of the Tahaa Lagoon

Fresh fish is pulled aboard as the LOST SOUL enters Raiatea

Jody checking out Bora Bora's
diving reef on Motu Tapu

Anchored off Sand Island in Suvarov

The main path on Suvarov

Bathtub Island on Suvarov in the Northern Cook Islands

Anchored in a small anchorage in Vavau, Tonga

Ali joined us while we were in Pago Pago and sailed with us to Tonga

Joel learning to eat Tongan style

Swallow cave in Tonga
Gee, wonder why they called it that

Braving a storm to make it to Oahu for Thanksgiving

A hitchhiker
joins us
mid-Pacific

Time for some R&R at the
Bel-Air hotel in Careyes, Mexico

Shopping for supplies in the Zihuatanejo *mercado*

Happy times. New Year's Eve in Acapulco

Not so happy times. In jail, Bahia Coco, Costa Rica

The aftermath of a very trying adventure, with the poster of the person I was supposed to be

Recuperation down the Costa Rica coast

The gates close in the Panama Canal

a picture on the inside cover of our MPC Boaters Directory phone book, we lined it up, and soon we were pulling into Twin Harbors, met by our friend Curt on his Maple Leaf 56, NAMAHANA.

We were home after over 20,000 miles. But as it would turn out, we would not be staying long.

We'd returned to civilization against our will because an old friend had offered to help me start a new cruising magazine. As we'd been cruising for awhile, we were about out of fun tickets, so the timing was right to return home and earn some more. What better way to do it than by creating a new magazine? Unfortunately, as we crossed the Pacific, my friend crossed over into another realm. He died of a heart attack during a meeting while I was enjoying a great cruise. This gave me much pause for thought. We were the same age, and if I had stayed, well, you know the old saying, "There but for the grace of God . . ."

So Jody and I immediately made plans for a hasty departure, before we fell into the great cesspool called civilization. It took less than three months, and we were gone. During those few months, the LOST SOUL had to put up with a lot of filming. First of all, they shot six episodes of *Hotel Malibu* at the marina we stayed in. It was like *Melrose Place* on the beach. Lots of sex, no plot, and not much similarity to real life.

Then, a bunch of perverts from Showtime shot a late-night movie called *The Island*. It had even less of a plot than *Hotel Malibu*, but more voluptuous bimbos. It was shot completely aboard the LOST SOUL and Captain Bitchin was last seen trying to find a copy of the video, which he still has not seen. Maybe you will see it, but don't let your kids watch!

Off to Greece

*T*here was a new face on board when the LOST SOUL departed Redondo Beach. Twenty-five-year-old Woody Henderson quit his job as bartender (he even looks a lot like Woody on Cheers) and joined up for the voyage for at least one year. While working on the boat, he was heard to mutter "What have I done?"

This time we decided we needed a little souvlaki. So where is the best souvlaki, you ask? In Sounion at a little taverna near the Temple of Poseidon. So it's off to Greece.

We actually made it out of the slip right on time. At 10:30 a.m. on October 25, we cast off the lines just as we threatened to do and were on our way.

The first leg was all of 24 miles to the Isthmus at Catalina where we spent one night saying goodbye to friends who worked there, and then we headed the whole 10 miles down Catalina Island to Avalon.

It was there that Jody and Woody were introduced to Parnelli Bitchin. We rented one of those electric golf carts and I had them white knuckled before we hit the bottom of the first long hill. It seems you can override the governor on those things downhill! Sometimes life is good.

Our friend, teacher Dave Bean, joined us for the trip to Cabo, and a little before 4 p.m. we said goodbye to the gang at the fuel dock and headed out for our first leg into foreign waters. A whopping 17 miles to the Coronado Islands in Mexico. We anchored an hour after dark and spent a great night under the stars.

The next day, we sailed in perfect weather with light winds and warm sunshine past Punta Banda and decided we'd stay in

Santo Tomás. As we pulled in, the winds whipped up to 28 miles an hour and started blowing stuff, like our brand new bean bag chair, off the boat. By the time we had everything under control we'd opted to anchor four miles further down the coast, and we dearly missed our bean bag.

It wasn't until the following day we found the real problem. It seems that something hit the autopilot when we were blown over. All of a sudden, we had no autopilot. Actually, it turned out to be rather nice; as we sailed the next few days we actually got to feel the boat.

One night, we tucked into the lee of the north shore at Cedros Island and listened to the sound of a hundred or so mating sea lions. As it got dark, the sea lion pups came out and started swimming around below the boat, and there was so much fluorescence in the water they left trails wherever they went. Talk about a flashback to the sixties!

We traded a six pack of brews for a six pack of lobster and, with a calico bass that Dave caught, we invited a couple from a near-by boat over for dinner. We dined on fresh ceviche, lobster in clam sauce over linguini, and fresh homemade wheat bread. In the morning, we had a perfect sail at eight knots for the 30 miles into Turtle Bay. It doesn't get any better.

Unfortunately, when things get to their best, it's usually downhill from there, and thus it happened that a few days later, after we spent a day at Isla Asuncion and a day at Santa Maria, the shit hit the fan.

The day started great. No winds and motoring on a calm sea. Then the winds started. But they started out of the south. The south? The winds never come from the south down here.

For the next 36 hours, we bucked against 30- to 35-knot winds directly on our nose. The seas built up, and before long we were getting knocked down to as low as 0.8 knot. That's less than one mile an hour.

Marvelous, simply marvelous.

What should have been a nice sail down to Cabo turned into the demented motor to hell. Eventually we cut right up to shore, in about 50 feet of water. From there we motored trying to hide in the lee of a non-existent point.

Once into Cabo, we pulled into the marina and it was like old home week. We ran into Mike who owns the cruisers' hideout, Latitude 22, while he was having a drink at the Baja Cantina.

We had "Short Wave" Dave fly down with a new autopilot. Two hours after he arrived, it was installed and time to go swimming. When we were in Hawaii, Dave had attained the name Short Wave Dave by surfing headfirst into the sand at Waimea Bay when there was a 15-foot shore break. He's still picking the sand out of his butt from that one.

Here in Cabo there was no shore break, in fact, there was no break at all, so we had the First Annual Short Wave Dave Cabo San Lucas Backward Body Surfing Championships. The way it worked was simple. You stand in water to your waist and wait until a wake from a passing boat goes by, then you flop on your back in the surf and let it wash you up on the beach. He who had the most sand in his or her shorts was the winner. Jody won, but she had more places to get sand stuck.

Dan the Slug Man flew in to sail with us for awhile. He'd helped sail the LOST SOUL back from Hawaii a few months earlier, and he was my mentor for awhile while I did a lot of the woodwork on the boat. After awhile, he became my tormentor, as he tried to drive me into a state of perfection. But since I was an ol' time biker, my training came through, and I managed to slop most of the work together, much to his chagrin.

Anyway, with Dan on board, we set sail at 5 a.m. for the 230-mile sail to Isla Isabella. From the time we set sail, we had about 20 knots of wind, and we sailed between nine and

11 knots for the next 20 hours. It was heaven. The wind was just aft of beam and was as steady as a wino at a free lunch.

We anchored at Isla Isabella and walked around checking out the mating frigate birds. The males had this big red bag they'd inflate on their throats to attract the women. Dan, Woody, and I tried it, but it just made Jody laugh, so we stopped.

We grabbed our snorkel gear and headed out to do some diving, and on our way we spotted some humpback whales. After shutting down the motor on the dinghy, we watched in awe as the four giant mammals drifted within 30 feet of us, just blowing steam and rolling in the warm waters of the Sea of Cortez.

In the morning, we headed out for Chacala, a small anchorage 57 miles south of Isabella. Once at anchor, we had a great dinner of fresh caught dorado and watched the fireflies cruise around us. We sat on the beach at a small palapa-type restaurant and downed some cold Pacificos, the local beer.

We almost regretted having to head into Puerto Vallarta, but it was nice talking with marina manager Karl over the VHF as we were coming in. It had been awhile since our last visit and he still remembered us. I don't know if that's a good or bad thing!

While we lavished in the great marina at Puerto Vallarta, we were joined by Jim Zietler, a powerboater who has sailed with us every trip we've made for the past five years or so. Chronologically, he's over 70, but mentally he's about on a par with me, somewhere in our teens. We always seem to have a good time. He signed on originally from Costa Rica to Panama, but then he added a leg from Puerto Vallarta for a week.

Sailing Mexico's Gold Coast

▶◀

We sailed to Yelapa as our first stop south of Puerto Vallarta. Yelapa is a small Indian village that has no roads to it. The only way in or out is by boat or over the mountains on a mule. The paths between the homes in the village cut up and down the hills and there are two waterfalls. It's unspoiled and beautiful. We spent a sunny day on the beach sipping cold Pacificos and eating pie. For years I've been going there, and for years there has been a family that sells pies on the beach. Apple pie, coconut pie, chocolate pie, even lemon meringue pie! And they are great. We munched down pieces of pies and ordered four whole pies to be delivered. At 6 p.m. sharp, a panga pulled up to the boat with pies hot from the oven.

The next day we sailed around the point to Ipala and anchored for a night, and then made the 54-mile sail south to Chamela. Chamela has the clearest water on the Pacific coast of Mexico, and we spent two days there snorkeling and anchored among the small islands in the bay. We met a couple who just completed a five-year circumnavigation of the world, and another couple just starting out on their first cruise. It's a small fraternity out here.

Then we entered paradise. Careyes. What a place! It's a small bay nestled among some islands in the middle of the Mexican Riviera. There's a Club Med and the Bel Air Hotel. Jody, Jim, and I spent a day lounging around the pool at the Hotel Careyes Bel Air, while Woody and his friend Shawn opted for the younger crowd at the Club Med.

After two days of decadence around the pool having food and drinks delivered to us, we figured we'd better get out. We were getting spoiled. In the morning, we hauled anchor and headed south once again, and soon we were sailing past Cabeza de Navidad.

It was here that my cruising coach, Alan Olsen, lost the STONE WITCH some 12 years earlier. He had hit a rock and the boat went down in less than 30 minutes. It felt more than just a little weird sailing over the same spot where such a great ship went down.

We dropped anchor in 18 feet of crystal blue water off the beach where my friend Philomena runs Los Pelicanos Restaurant, and is the unofficial mother of all cruisers. I hadn't seen her in six years, but in a matter of minutes, it felt as if we had come home. We sat there all day trading stories with Philomena and a friend, John, who owns Juanito's Hamburgers near Las Hadas in Manzanillo. It was a most comfortable day. If you ever sail to Barra de Navidad, stop and visit Philomena.

Las Hadas in Manzanillo is pure decadence. I can think of no better way to kill some time. We anchored about 50 yards off the beach which was lined with small white palapas. This is where the movie *10* was filmed, and it lives up to its movie reputation. We met Denise and Terrance on MOUNTAIN OYSTER who had just sailed up from Belize via Panama, and we gave them hints on what was in front of them, while they gave us hints as to what we could look forward to on our trip.

One of the highlights of our stay was when we went with the crew of MOUNTAIN OYSTER and Peter, a South African on FEATHERBED, to a festival for the Virgin of Guadeloupe. There's a small town just at the bottom of the hill below Las Hadas called Agua Dulce. We saw some activity and stopped to check it out. They had a large fireworks display set up, and they needed some help to lift it into place. The children crowded around me because of my size and tattoos and asked me to help. We lifted it into place and then the town adopted us for the night. We were surrounded by the children all night as they asked questions about where we came from, and told us of their town. It was a beautiful experience that none of us will forget.

But let's get back to reality. We hoisted anchor and set out for the south once again. Our first overnight stop was at Cabeza Negra (How's that for a romantic name? It means "Blackhead") and we found out what rock 'n' roll was all about. We rocked and rolled all night as we sat abeam to the Pacific swells coming in.

Then we got real lucky. We anchored at Bahia Maruata. It's right out of a travelogue. A large, white sand beach, palm trees, scattered large rocks, and small islands with caves so large you can actually go through them in your dinghy, and a picturesque little village with about 50 people who live off the sea. When we landed at the beach, there were about 30 buzzards splitting up some fish that the locals had just cleaned, and the dogs had a ball chasing them. A couple of old ladies sat doing their laundry in a stream, and it was so peaceful you just wanted to scream.

The next morning's sail started out with a 20-pound dorado, which we hauled in with care, and soon Woody was making fillets out of it on the foredeck. Then, we got a real strike on the pole. Woody and I took turns yelling "Wahoo!" and trying to reel it in. When we finally got it aboard, after about 45 minutes, it turned out to be about a 70-pound wahoo. When it was cleaned, we had over 20 steaks and a whole lot of fillets. We actually had to pull in our lines because we'd run out of room in the freezer.

A few days later, we arrived in Ixtapa, where we bounced from the marina to Isla Grande and back, and waited for Juanita and Jack to show up. They would be with us from Ixtapa / Zihuatanejo to Acapulco, about 120 miles south.

While we were in Marina Ixtapa, we were constantly seeing signs telling us to watch out for alligators. The swamp they dredged the marina out of was once the home to a lot of these prehistoric looking fellas. In particular was one named George, who liked to prowl through the marina in the evenings looking for a stray dog or a small child. The day Junita and Jack showed up we saw poor George, the rampaging six-foot alligator. It must have been humiliating for him. He was all trussed up in the back of a pickup truck on his way to the local butcher.

The day before Christmas, we sailed seven miles south to the bay in Zihuatanejo. Here we found the fleet, all the boats we'd seen coming down the coast, about 40 anchored sailboats, all waiting out the holidays. For the next couple of days we swam and relaxed, exploring the old town.

It was in Zihuatanejo that the boats were built that Juan Cabrillo used when he discovered California. It was hard to imagine that this town was already old when California was first sighted by the Spanish. The marketplace, *mercado central*, is in the same location it has been for hundreds of years, and it seemed strange sitting at a counter where Juan Cabrillo might have sat on his way to discover California.

After Christmas, once again we took off on our journey. We spent one night in a rolly anchorage just south of Zihuatanejo and discovered another truth about cruising. Don't sleep out on deck in an anchorage that has a swamp near it. I realized this in the morning as I was scratching a few of the over 100 mosquito bites I had. I had more bites than a midget referee at a giant dog fight. It's not all fun and games out here! For the next couple days, we sailed, rubbed Calamine lotion on our bites, and generally scratched our way to Acapulco.

We first sighted Acapulco from about 40 miles out at sea. It looked like a jeweled city. The lights covered the hillsides and the crystal clear sky showed the city off to its best advantage. As dawn approached, we entered the harbor and headed over to the Acapulco Yacht Club. Fortunately, it was filled to capacity, so we had to go the new La Marina Acapulco a few hundred meters north.

La Marina Acapulco is the home of the beautiful people of Mexico. It is a private club with a marina that is filled with million-dollar boats and has a great swimming pool that overlooks the marina and the bay. We got to know Alex, the manager, who is from Argentina, and he gave us a pass to get into the private area of the marina. I never knew there were so many millionaires in Mexico, the distributor for Coke, the world's largest banana exporter, and a whole lot more. The facilities are the best that I have seen in Mexico. They have 24-hour security, clean docks, and the people are really helpful. They did all of our paper clearance and even arranged fuel for us. It's the new cruising center for Acapulco as far as I'm concerned.

On New Year's Eve, our crew consisted of myself, Jody and Woody, Woody's girlfriend Holly, and Tom Sullivan, who would be sailing with us to Costa Rica. Tom, Jody, and I joined four folks from MAINE SAIL (they were originally from Maine) and we went to a beachfront restaurant for the evening. When we arrived they were playing a song we'd never heard before, but would be hearing for years to come. It was called the macarena. As we sat at our table we noticed that some folks were kind of moving to the music. The next time we looked around everybody in the place was dancing, on table tops, on the bar, wherever. It was real weird.

After dinner we sat and downed some tequila and enjoyed a great evening. At about midnight the fireworks started. We were pretty impressed. It seemed like they were right on top of us.

In fact, they were breaking *on* our heads. Large gops of burning sulphur were dropping into our drinks and sizzling. As was our hair. Large burning balls of sulphur sprinkled the crowds, and it was like being inside the fireworks. Only in Mexico could this happen.

We found Acapulco to be very expensive, but it was a great place to stock up for the next leg of our trip. We had Anita from Redondo fly in to Acapulco on the evening of the first, and then we were off.

We made an overnight passage to Punta Galera about 135 miles south, and anchored one night there. It was pretty and desolate. Woody and Holly went ashore on his kayak and were attacked by a gaggle of long-eared Brahman cattle. They were okay until Holly "eeeked." They wanted to investigate what all the "eeeking" was about and started to amble in their direction. This, in Holly's estimation, was an attack, so they departed the beach at a full trot.

We stayed in Puerto Escondido a few days. The crew lived up to the LOST SOUL image, stumbling home from the disco near 4 a.m. after searching for Anita's lost shoes and purse.

The next morning at about 6:30 a.m., I felt, rather than heard, a dull thud. What I heard was the aft anchor line separating. We donned our scuba gear and managed to find it and get it aboard. Then we headed east to Puerto Angel, which lies on the end of the Gulf of Tehuantepec. This sea is notorious for winds up to 100 miles per hour coming off the land. If there is a high in the Gulf of Mexico it shoots across Mexico here, at its most narrow point.

As we sat in Escondido, a boat came in that had its mainsail ripped and its headsail destroyed. It had just come across the Tehuantepec.

Just what you don't want to see.

Upon our entry to Puerto Angel, we were greeted by a boat filled with Mexican Navy. Two youngsters with Uzi machine guns and two officers, who proceeded to go through the boat with a fine-toothed comb. They seemed really upset when they didn't find anything. What do I look like, a gun runner?

We spent a day in Puerto Angel. We did a couple of chores on the boat and at about 10 a.m., we headed ashore to a beautiful little beach with some palapa restaurants. We settled at a table in the sand at the surf line under the shade of a palapa, and the waiter started to bring stuff. I love it when waiters bring stuff.

He started by bringing us an order of huevos rancheros. This cost us six pesos. That's about $1.25. Then we started to drink a few cold Dos Equis beers and we were joined by John, a singlehander off another boat. We started talking boats and cruising, and soon we had the five people in our crew along with John sitting around downing cold brews, and realized it was lunch time, so we ordered some shrimp (15 pesos, or $3). We sat there until the afternoon, took our dinghy out to the boat, did some reading and swimming, and then, after a great dinner of the fish we'd caught on the way down, settled in for movie night onboard. Wasted day? I don't think so!

The next day, we motored out and headed toward Huatulco, our last planned port in Mexico. About two miles before the entrance, we saw an inviting beach tucked behind a small island. We ducked in to check it out and stumbled upon Bahia Cacaluta. It's not on any of our cruising guides or charts, and it is absolutely the most beautiful place we've seen in Mexico.

Jody had tears in her eyes because she couldn't stand how great this place was. She does that. There is a virgin, white beach that runs about a mile, ending in a small, blue swimming hole. At the other end is a freshwater lagoon just behind the sand dunes, and a small sand beach between some rocks with the bluest water we'd seen so far. It's heaven, and only two miles from Huatulco.

In Huatulco it got even better. This has got to be the best part of Mexico's Pacific coast. More small cozy beaches. Shrimp ceviche for 20 pesos (about $4) and beers for under a dollar.

The highlight of my stay was when I awoke to a full-body massage by crew lady Anita, a professional masseuse who sailed with us from Acapulco to Huatulco. Two hours of pure heaven. It was time to head out into the Gulf of Tehuantepec, and across the 660 miles past Guatemala, El Salvador, Nicaragua, and into Costa Rica for our next leg.

Guatemalan Speed Bumps

We hit a little wind as we entered the Tehuantepec and then it started to die. Before we'd gone 100 miles, we were motoring. We had a singlehander named Dean aboard PASSAPORTE in front of us, and a 150-foot powerboat named ENCHANTER passing us as we left. You may remember it as the boat they used in the opening of the movie *Clear and Present Danger*. After setting a time to meet on the sideband radio, all three boats took off. In the morning, we were pretty spread out. The powerboat was way in front, we were in the middle, and PASSAPORTE was behind. The farther we got into the gulf, the less wind we had. All the stories we'd heard about crossing the Tehuantepec, all the tension, and then, nothing. Our second day out, we caught a 150-pound sailfish (yeah, we got pictures to prove it!) and then we had a large mahi-mahi break our line. The fish are big because it's so hard for the fishermen to get out there with the storms that come up so fast.

As midnight of the second day passed, we entered Guatemalan waters. The weather stayed unbelievably beautiful as we sailed out of Mexico, through Guatemala, El Salvador, past Honduras, and almost through Nicaragua. During the passage, we encountered a whole bunch of what we started to call Guatemalan speed bumps.

Guatemalan speed bumps are giant sea turtles. I've been told that these guys are endangered, and now I know why. Damn things can't get out of their own way. All night long you keep hearing, "Bump," "Bang," "Thump."

Don't go getting all ecological on me now. We didn't kill any, just caused a lot of headaches. We must have bumped into 10 to 15 during our crossing of the Tehuantepec. Even during the day, by the time you see the silly things, it's too late.

The Gulf of Tehuantepec is the western side of the point where Central America is at its narrowest. They have storms that come suddenly out of the north, called "tehuantepecers," and storms that come out of the east, called "papagayos."

We got hit by a papagayo storm starting at about 5 a.m. on the final day of our crossing. The winds started at about 15 knots, and by the time they reached 20 we started to put in our first reef on the mainsail. When it hit 30 we put in the second reef and reefed the mizzen. At 35 we reefed our headsail and when it hit 40 we pulled in the headsail and dropped the mizzen. For the next 40 miles, we battled into 15-foot seas and up to 50 mile an hour winds, trying to make the coast of Costa Rica. We had to turn downwind for awhile, and instead of our first planned anchorage, we opted for one that would protect us from the big seas and gale force winds.

We made it into Papagayo Bay and snuck in behind a hill. The winds whipped over our heads at up to 55 knots, but it was calm where we anchored. We ended up anchoring three times as the wind whipped around us. Dean on PASSAPORTE was still out in it, and we talked with him twice a day to monitor his position. He was alone, and being blown farther and farther out to sea.

In the morning, we motored through winds over 55 miles an hour for five miles to a more protected anchorage, Potrero Grande, and finally felt as if we were in Costa Rica. A rain forest backed the white sand beach and tropical birds were abundant. We spent a good night there and then we had a great sail across Papagayo Bay in reducing winds to a place called Bahia Huevos.

Of course Dean on PASSAPORTE wasn't having as much fun. He was still being blown around.

Meanwhile we were sitting in a deep bay with white sand beaches, deep blue waters and a river mouth. We got to play National Geographic explorers as we took our dinghy almost three miles up the river into deep rain forest and swampland. We saw sea snakes, eagles, cranes, and herons. In the afternoon of our second day, we explored caves and tidepools. We sailed five miles to Bahia Coco, the first small town in Costa Rica.

After checking in with the port captain, we had another small world story. At the Bahia Bar & Yacht Club the lady who came out to take our order was Penny. She and Paul, her husband, used to own the Galleon in Avalon, our favorite restaurant back on Catalina Island. Now, after sailing almost 3,000 miles, they are making burgers on the beach in Costa Rica.

We went ashore and had T-bone steak dinners at the best restaurant in town, and then dropped in at the Bahia Yacht Club for a brew and to exchange Yacht Club burgees. There was a fiesta in town, and the whole town was out in force. I have never felt so at home in such a short time. That feeling was soon to change, drastically. We almost hated to leave to go back to the boat to run the generator. In fact, our crew, Tom and Woody, stayed ashore that night.

When Jody and I got back to the boat, we were surrounded by birds. Hundreds of them. Cute little finches. Cute until we realized they were using my boat for a toilet! They'd taken up residence as we ate dinner ashore. There had to be over 200 to 300 of them in, and on, the boat. It took us a half-hour to get the damn things off, and out, of the boat. The last few we ended up picking up by hand and setting outside, since they couldn't find their way out without bumping into the portholes, head first. Then, it took us another hour to get all the bird guano off the boat. It was during this cleaning spree that we found our gecko. We've had pet gecko lizards on board since Tahiti. They eat bugs and are cute. We had lost track of them since mid-December, but found a baby gecko on board the night of the birds.

In the morning, we talked with Dean again, and he was really getting worried. The seas were up over 30 feet and the winds were blowing at up to 50 knots. He was still over 70 miles out of Costa Rica and losing ground.

A Free Trip to Prison

*I*t all started when I went to clear customs. I walked into the customs office and the next thing I knew, I was being locked up in a six-by-six, dark concrete cell with a steel door and a smell somewhat akin to that found in your everyday Costa Rican outhouse. No one spoke English there, my Spanish was not the best, and I couldn't figure out what I'd done. A few hours later Tom, Jody, and Woody had contacted the U.S. consul and were told, "It's a matter of Costa Rican national security and there's nothing we can do."

Soon, they got a lawyer and after a couple hours of me counting cockroaches he let us know he'd been told it was "too big" for him to handle, and to drop it. He was almost as mad as I was, but not quite.

At sunset, after spending a lovely day amongst drunks and perverts (and those were the guards!), I was handcuffed and placed between two guys in civilian clothes, armed with Uzis, in the back seat of a Bronco, with another man driving and a third sitting backwards in the front seat with a loaded and cocked Uzi pointing at me. I was figuring it was all over as they drove me out of Playa del Coco and headed off on a dirt road into the jungle. The humor quickly deteriorated an hour later as we pulled up in front of the federal prison in Liberia. This was not a fun-looking place. High walls and a large, foreboding set of steel doors with a bunch of Third World commandos standing around with beer bellies and Uzis. Once inside, they sat me down and everybody in the place was looking at me. Guess they never saw a 6'4", 350-pound tattooed weirdo before.

I was busy trying to see which group of the few hundred

guys in there had plans to be my personal proctologists when two CIA guys showed up. How did I know they were CIA? Izod shirts, crew cuts, dark glasses, and white socks with loafers. They were in uniform! I have never been so happy to see anyone in my life. I told them how glad I was to see them, and all they said was "Shut the fuck up!" Nice guys, huh? Your tax dollars at work. I was taken down the corridor to the "interrogation room" which was a large room with a pool table (and just where did they think they were going to stick those pool balls?) and little table/chair combos like you had in grade school. Now try to picture El Largo Bitchin squished into one of those little things, with handcuffs on, still in my swimming trunks.

The CIA guys explained that they had flown in to identify me and take me back to the States. "For what?" I asked, wide-eyed and innocent. "Well, let's see," one of the escapees from a Happy Days commercial said, "how does escaping prison and being one of the 10 most wanted men in America sound?"

At the time it wasn't really sounding too good.

They started asking me questions like where did I get my phony passport and other neat CIA stuff. We played James Bond for about an hour with me sitting in the middle of the large room stuffed into the mini-chair, while these guys got to practice all their cop stuff, and then another man came in. His name was Fred and he was with the FBI. He'd just gotten off a plane from Miami and had the fingerprints of the guy I was supposed to be. He was really pissed at me because I screwed up his weekend by making him fly out to Costa Rica. I apologized and promised never to do it again.

Then he broke out the description and a wanted poster. The guy was 5'11". I'm 6'4". He weighed 160 pounds. My weenie weighs more than that! He had an eagle tattooed on his right arm. I have the Harley-Davidson logo, with wings, as do about 1,157,874 other people. They fingerprinted me, on a neat little portable, digital fingerprint fax machine and I sat there for the next hour playing like I didn't really care what the fax they sent would reveal. I was actually starting to think I might be guilty. Back in Washington D.C. they were checking the prints, and when they were through they sent a fax. Guess what? I wasn't the dude.

No shit! I could have told em that. Then all the grumpy Costa Ricans who'd been holding me all day were soon smiling at me and calling me amigo. It wasn't their fault, they were told by the American consul that I was a bad dude who'd escaped prison. They thought I was *muy malo*.

The only good thing that came out of the day was all of the Americans in town who did everything in their power to help Jody and the crew get me out. Great people. But all in all it did take the edge off an otherwise fun stay in Bahia Coco. That night we attended the fiesta in town. I had beers with the locals who'd had me in jail all day, and generally tried to get the feeling of a dirty cell off me. It was at this time that Jody said she had been told by the lawyer that I was being kidnapped and flown back to the States by the FBI because they have no extradition in Costa Rica and that's the way they do it there. Boy, would that have capped off a great day!

The next day, we took Paul, Penny, and some of the local folks sailing to celebrate my release, and then things got back to normal. But Dean was still out in it, and it was getting worse. He'd been out there now for 10 days, and had run out of fuel. He was drifting about 30 miles a day away from Costa Rica. He'd made it to within 40 miles and then been washed back to over 170 miles out.

Doing the Ditch

W e changed crew at the marina of Bahia Flamingo.
We dropped off Tom Sullivan and picked up John
and Sue Fisher, Jim Zietler, and his friend Greg. It was blowing stink as we filled our fuel tanks and we decided to head
south and get out of it. But there was no getting out of it.

We talked with Dean again on PASSAPORTE and he was not
having fun. He'd called in for assistance and the Coast Guard
in Boston (Boston?) picked up the call. They launched some
Navy search planes out of Panama and found the boat still
afloat, and tried to drop him some fuel. He said he would be
able to make it in, but the seas were still at 30 feet and the
winds were still blowing a full gale, and he hadn't slept in almost four days.

The next day we overheard an Air Force jet from Panama
that had responded to Dean's Mayday call. They had a vessel
on its way to him, and had dropped him fuel. He was still
fighting the papagayo, and we never heard from him again. We
were told he eventually sailed back to Mexico after turning
around, limping back up the coast.

We arrived at Bahia Carrillo. The wind stopped as we
rounded the cape, and it was calm as we entered the bay.
There's a hotel on a hill overlooking the bay, a reef that has
large breakers rolling across it all day and night, and calm anchorage. We spent the next day swimming, playing with our
pool toys, and generally loafing and soaking up the sun.

Hey, good news! Some hippies did escape! We arrived in
a beautiful bay called Bahia Bellena and on one of the most
beautiful beaches we've seen this trip, was a family who were
throwbacks to the 60s. Her name was Honey and he was

Heart. They had sailed down in the early 70s on a trimaran that is still anchored in the sheltered bay. Their nine kids (well, there's not a lot to do in paradise!) were running around in blue water, white sand, and palm trees. We spent the day ashore with our hammocks hung from the palms, playing with their dogs, and swimming. The squirrels and mynah birds were everywhere.

We sailed south to Drake's Bay, where we found crystal blue waters, clear rivers, friendly people, and beautiful scenery. We spent a couple of days there. Andy, who sailed with me in Mexico and once to the South Pacific, has a place in Drake's, and he came and met us on the beach. On Jody's birthday, horses were rented to take a jungle trek. As it turns out, the horses couldn't even get through the jungle, so the intrepid explorers ended up neck deep in jungle rivers. That night we had dinner at the Eagle and Bear Wilderness Lodge where Cookie fixed up a birthday feast for eight, including champagne, and a birthday cake for Jody.

After having too much fun at Drake's Bay, Andy joined us for the sail to Golfito, where we were to check out of Costa Rica. We got there in the afternoon, did our checkout, and spent the night. At sunup, we were heading into Panama.

Just before sunset, we came to a small group of rocks called Islas Ladrones, which means Islands of Thieves. We tucked in behind these isolated rocks and watched a beautiful sunset. At midnight all hell broke lose as we were hit with a squall. We traded anchor watches and at 5 a.m., an hour before dawn, we set sail again, on to Bahia Honda.

Bahia Honda turned out to be a great stopover where we found plenty of white sand beaches with no people. Once again in the a.m. we took off for Las Perlas Islands off the Canal Zone. We sailed in great weather, south, out of Honda, then made some easterly toward Punta Mala and rounded the point at about 11 p.m. "Mala" means bad. It deserves that name. Before we passed it, the wind turned strong, and it freshened as we came around. Through the night and the next day we motor-sailed again in 25- to 30-knot winds and short, choppy seas.

At about 2 p.m. we headed into our night's anchorage at Isla San Jose. Keeping in mind the extensive tidal range, we anchored and dropped the dinghy to go explore the shore. It was unbelievably beautiful. We had a great dinner of mahi mahi and turned in to catch up on our sleep.

At 12:35 a.m., all hell broke loose. I awoke to the sound of a loud crunch and I felt the boat shudder. It had the sound of 42 tons of teak and fiberglass hitting solid rock. We'd dragged anchor during the night and come down hard on a huge rock. As there was an 18-foot tide in that area of the Pacific, the 30-foot water we anchored in was now 12 feet deep. Normally okay, but in this case, we'd pulled back a few feet also, and landed on some rocks. As we were getting away from the rock in the pitch black night, we slammed into another rock, this time on the bottom. The first was on the rudder. It was dark and blowing about 25 knots as we felt our way out between the rocks of the small harbor. Partially using the sail by Braille method, we made it into the open bay. In the next two hours, we anchored three more times. The first in 25 feet of water with 175 feet of chain. It dragged. Then in 30 feet of water with 250 feet of chain. We dragged again. Finally, we anchored in 25 feet of water with 350 feet of chain. That's a 14-1 ratio, and it held, but we kept an anchor watch on all night.

In the morning, I dove to check out the damage. We had a chunk about three inches wide and a foot long ground out of the rear of the rudder, and a large chunk about six inches wide and three feet long along the bottom of the keel. None of the damage was structural. Also, while we were re-anchoring the third time, Dolly the Dolphin, our monkeypod figurehead, broke her arm. It looks like she'll have it in a cast for awhile.

Then came our introduction to the Panama Canal. What a ditch! It was unbelievable. My old friend Keith Ball, editor of *Easyriders* magazine, flew in to join us for the canal crossing. After we picked up a mooring at the Balboa Yacht Club, we went inside and found a great place to have some cool brew. The local brew there is called Panama and it isn't too bad. It's also cheap, which puts it high on my shopping list.

The next day Keith, Jody, Woody, and I met a cabbie named Franklin. He'd been born in the canal area 67 years ago and knew more about it than anyone. He took us to the old section, where the buildings are piled on top of each other and made of wood, and have been waiting for over 200 years for a fire to clear it out. Then, we went to Old Panama. Here, I entered a state of grace, as I was on the spot where Captain Henry Morgan stood as he burned the city to the ground in the 1600s. The remains of the buildings still stand as a monument. Being an amateur pirate myself, I was entranced.

Meanwhile, John, Sue, Jim, and Greg explored the other side of Panama. They had lunch at a five-star restaurant and an air-conditioned ride around town. Our heap was a 1974 Ford with windows that wouldn't roll up. Each group had a ball. Then it was time to do the canal.

As our boat measured over 68 feet overall (they even count the dinghy hanging off the back), we were assigned a pilot. Any boat under 65 feet can go through with a guide, but over that you get a pilot. It costs the same, so I felt better with a full-fledged pilot on board. He showed us where to go, and soon we were inside the first lock tied to a tug that was going through. The water started to boil around us like hot water surrounds a lobster, and I couldn't help but compare the two situations. Soon, we were looking off our aft deck to the canal, some 85 feet below us! We made it through the two Miraflores locks and the Pedro Miguel locks. Then, we were motoring through the Gaillard Cut, where hundreds of men lost their lives digging the canal.

We motored out onto Gatun Lake and got to spend the night anchored there, awaiting our descent through the Gatun locks the next day. If you go slow enough through the canal you get to spend the night on the lake. It's a real treat.

That evening, we swam in the fresh water of Lake Gatun, 87 feet above sea level and I got to run my generator and all the other motors using fresh water to clear the salt out of the lines.

In the morning, we went into the locks first. As we sent our lines up the walls to the linehandlers, I looked behind me, and here came a 500-foot rust bucket, belching black smoke and bearing down on me. He was to be our lock partner. Yech!

Each new lock was great, as we pulled to the end and looked out over the waters way below us. Then, they emptied the lock, and we were a step closer to sea level. We motored out to the bay in front of Colón and anchored.

Once in the Panama Canal Yacht Club, we made a discovery. Don't go to town. It seems that they have a 60 percent unemployment rate, and there are gangs of people out there mugging anyone who walks the streets. Keith and I walked about a mile to make a phone call, and it looked like a war zone. Burned-out cars and trashed, empty streets past buildings that had been burned out. This was the old American section of Colón, and they say it takes about 30 days for the Panamanians to trash a building once it's turned over. In downtown Colón, they were rioting and we heard gunshots all through the night. We spent the next three days waiting for a crew change, as Jim, Greg, and Keith were flying out and new folks were coming in.

Out Into the Caribbean

*I*t was with no great feeling of loss that we hauled our dirt-encased anchor and headed out of the Panama breakwater into the Caribbean. Our crew for this leg consisted of John and Sue Fisher, still with us from Costa Rica, Neil McNeil, who'd flown in to Panama to join us, along with my well-endowed sidekick Jody, and crewman Woody.

As we headed north into the deep blue Caribbean, we were greeted with 25 knots of head wind on the nose and seas running between 10 to 12 feet, but it still felt clean and good after the slime pit called Colón. For the next 30 hours, we motorsailed into the wind and seas, and when we were about 15 miles out of San Andrés we were finally able to sail, and sail we did, doing about eight knots!

Our arrival in San Andrés Island, Colombia, was a surprise for all of us. All we'd ever heard about Colombia was that it was full of drug dealers and thieves. Well, it was about as beautiful an island as I've seen. Brilliant blue and green waters over white sand and a protective reef surrounding the anchorage.

I was a little surprised to see high-rise buildings and casinos, but we soon found out that this Colombian outpost is a haven to the drug cartels from all over the world. Crime is almost unheard of here. Large custom-built homes surround the island, and as our taxi driver Jimmy informed us, they are for the cartels from Turkey, Greece, China, Spain, and Hong Kong, as well as Colombia. The town was clean and well run, if not just a little on the expensive side. In Panama a dish of chicken and rice was about U.S. $3. In San Andrés, you could expect to pay over U.S. $10 for the same thing. We did get to do some sightseeing while there, and we found a large cave filled with fresh water used by Captain Henry Morgan as a water source when he was anchored here preparing to raid Panama. We saw no Americans, but found the people to be very friendly to us, and U.S. music was everywhere we went.

Neil was awarded the "Plan Ahead" award while anchored in San Andrés. It seems that while the rest of us were off snorkeling on a beautiful little motu near the anchorage, Neil, who had stayed on board, decided to do a little swimming. He dove off the boat. Unfortunately, he forgot to lower the boarding ladder.

Yeah, you got it. He swam around the boat four or five times like a turd in a punch bowl, and finally signaled a neighboring boat who launched their dinghy and picked him up, so he could get aboard LOST SOUL from their dinghy. We got a lot of mileage out of that during dinner that night.

We made a rough two-day crossing to a small reef just above the Nicaragua border called Media Luna Reef. We searched for a place to hide out of the swells to get some sleep and all we could find was a small white sand island less than 200 feet long and 50 feet wide. We anchored in its lee for a good night's rest. Or so we thought.

Just as the sun set, a boat approached us. Now we had been warned in San Andrés that some Nicaraguans were robbing U.S. boats near their borders, and we were just four miles from their border. The approaching boat had no running lights, and put a spotlight on us as they anchored. For the next 12 hours we stood "anchor watch" with a loaded 12-gauge shotgun at the ready.

In the morning, we found out we were still alive and unrobbed so we hoisted anchor and headed out for a small reef called Vivorillo. We made it almost eight miles before the winds and seas started to knock us backwards. We decided to turn around and go back to our little reef with the robbers. In the daylight the other boat wasn't as menacing, and that night we slept a little better as we sat out the storm behind this little cay.

The next day we took off again, and this time we had a lot better luck. By midday, we had a great sail going, as we headed toward Guanaja, Honduras. Guanaja is a small island just east of Roatán, and the settlement is pretty damned unique. The town is located on a small cay about one-half mile off Settlement Cay, and it is covered with homes and businesses. So many, in fact, most of them were built on stilts over the water. The walkways are overhung with signs of the businesses, and there are no streets. The businesses just haul their stuff in on three-wheeled bicycles down the sidewalks. As we landed to clear with the officials, kids milled around wanting to be our guides. We picked one and he stuck to us like glue for the two days we stayed, helping us with the port captain, with getting fruits and vegetables and just generally being there.

Also we met a man from Tennessee who'd lived there for the last 23 years on a small islet off the cay. He had a dive resort that he'd set up when he'd retired, and we ended up staying on a mooring he had there for the next two days, diving at his resort, and enjoying home cooked meals. Two wrecks at 60 feet and a sea wall that was unreal made the diving spectacular.

We headed out one morning for Barbareta Island, about 13 miles away. It was just like Gilligan's Island, but the castaways consisted of two Hondurans. They had been stranded for 10 days. It seems they had paddled over from the mainland to do some fishing and get away from their wives. While there, one had cut his foot pretty bad, and they were stuck. They were out of food and had been living on rainwater and a soup made from the small crabs on the beach. It was a 13-mile row in their dugout canoes to get back to the mainland. We gave them some medicine and helped clean up the cut on the man's foot. We gave them some food and water. When they saw the can of Spam we'd brought, they acted as if it was a roast or something. Guess when you've been living on saltwater crab soup, it might seem like a gourmet delight. Of course, they insisted on trading us some shells for the food. We felt we got the best of the deal.

The best feeling you can get while cruising is helping someone who really needs it. We knew they appreciated the hand, but what was really touching was when Jody went back to the boat and brought them a pack of cigarettes. I swear, I saw tears in the eyes of one man. He went back to the lean-to they'd built and got a shell. It was a beautiful small conch shell, and it had been polished by hand. He handed it to Jody with both hands, bowing slightly, and you could see it had great value to him.

It now resides in a place of honor on the LOST SOUL.

The next day, as we were sailing past Fantasy Island off the coast of Roatán, we heard a call on the radio and we came on with some info the person wanted. It turned out to be Dan, a man I'd met eight years earlier in Hawaii while cruising there, and now he was on a new boat called RAPID TRANSIT. He was delivering it to Cabo San Lucas. We made plans to meet at the entrance to Fantasy Island, where he would lead us in. He did so and we had a great day diving the reef. Later we went drinking into the night at the French Harbor Yacht Club.

After our hangovers became manageable the next day, Dan left for the Panama Canal, and we headed to the west end of Roatán to await nightfall, for the next leg of our journey. At 10 p.m. we raised anchor and headed west, for an overnight passage to Glover's Reef in Belize.

When we pulled in we found a pristine white coral island surrounded by a hundred or so shades of green and blue water. We anchored in 12 feet of crystal clear *agua* and were soon swimming to a virgin white sand beach. Awhile later, we went snorkeling on an isolated reef in the lagoon, and then it was back to the boat.

The next day we sailed north to a place called Lighthouse Reef. Once again, unbelievable! There are three wrecked ships on the reef to guide you in, and warn you to be careful. Then you pick up a mooring.

Okay, so I'm not real original, but Belize will take the originality right out of you. It is beauty wherever you look. About a half million colors of blue surround a white sand beach backed by a rich jungle, untouched, as it is a natural preserve set aside by the Belize government. The lighthouse keeper on the island was a Rastafarian named Frank, and he joined us with his three-year-old son, Wassan, for dinner on the boat. Nice people, and a great island.

In the morning we dove and snorkeled around the reef. About midday, our mooring line separated with a bang and we decided it would be better to head out than to drop an anchor. We headed around the reef and picked up another mooring at Long Cay, about six miles west, where we spent another star-filled night on the reefs of Belize. The next day we sailed up to Northern Cay on Lighthouse Reef and did some more diving and had a few cocktails at the dive resort there. We spent an easy night at anchor, and readied ourselves for the next day, when we'd sail for Mexico.

It started at dawn as we picked our way out of the shallow pass and into the deep blue. We hadn't been motoring more than five minutes when we doused the engine and started our record sail. For the next six hours we never did under eight knots, at times reaching 10 knots.

The 54-mile crossing from Lighthouse Reef to Xcalak in Mexico took us all of five and a half hours. But it got fun as we approached the 75-foot wide pass into the reef at Xcalak. It seems that the 20-knot winds that pushed us there also built up some 10- to 15-foot seas, and they were breaking as we entered the reef, through that little bitty hole in the reef they laughingly called a pass.

The fun continued as we were surfing through this little hole in a 42-ton boat. Now that was exciting, especially as we watched the depth meter read 30-20-15-10, and, well, you get the picture. I don't know if I was the biggest wreck, or my crew, who stood transfixed waiting for the crash.

It didn't come, at least not yet. We made the pass and turned north into the lagoon trying to find a place to anchor, but the depth sounder must have been wrong. It couldn't really be just eight feet in here, could it?

Well, actually no, it wasn't. It was six feet, *and we draw eight feet!*

You got it. We went up on the reef. Grounded out. For the first time in over 55,000 miles of sailing, I grounded.

They say you haven't been cruising till you've done it. I guess now I can say I was cruising! For the next hour, the six of us, and Bill from a Catalina 38 called MARAUDER, worked at getting the 42-ton LOST SOUL off the bottom. We were jammed hard. First, we tried to back her off, then to go forward. We attached a line to the top of our halyard and tried to pull her over. We took our storm hook and set it 300 feet into the deeper water, and tried to kedge off. Finally, we tried all of the above, and also raised all of our sails and pushed with the two dinghies. We did it! Damn, did we feel good as we set our hook and invited Bill and his lady over for some chili, wine, and talk about getting large boats off shallow bottoms. What a trip! It really brought the crew together. They worked so well together, you'd think they had rehearsed. It's times like that which make you feel alive.

But the next day was the real "E" ticket ride. It made that day look like child's play. It started after we had checked into Mexico, as this was our first port on the Caribbean side of Mexico. Clearance was easy and we finished by 10 a.m. the next day. After a five-minute walk through the dusty village, where we saw the five residents who lived there, two of which were dogs, Jody and I headed back to the boat. The rest of the crew went ashore and after a five-minute walk were ready to return to the boat also. There was nothing in the town to look at. Not even a bar or restaurant. The wind had whipped up to over 40 knots and the seas were breaking well over the reef. Inside, it started to get lumpy, and we were just a foot off the bottom. As the swell grew and we started to bounce on the bottom, we had only one chance, and that was to get out of there and head up to Chinchorro Bank, a reef about 40 miles north. We headed toward the place where we entered the reef the day before. The winds were blowing at about 40 knots and the seas had kicked up to 11 to 15 feet. But it wasn't the seas that bothered me. It was the surf. Full on 15- to 18-foot break-ing waves were coming in the narrow pass.

I decided we should go for it. We lined up the hole in the reef with the lighthouse and headed out into the pass. As we hit it, a wave broke over the whole boat, filling our aft state-room with sea water, as we had left the aft hatch open. Who expected waves this big? I spun the wheel from port to star-board trying to hold her straight into the waves and plunged the throttle to full, pushing it up to 2,500 rpm. Usually I would be doing about nine and a half knots at that rpm but we were standing still.

Standing still? At full throttle? The LOST SOUL lurched up into a wave and then had another break over her. The seas were high and close, and the boat sea-horsed up and down as the seas continued to break over us. The depth sounder read from a high of 28 feet to a low of six feet. We managed to keep from bottoming out but I don't know how. It seemed like hours, but actually it took about 20 minutes to get through the surf and out into the sea. That was the longest 20 minutes of my life!

What a thrill! Everyone was high as we broke out of the surf and into the open sea. We raised the mainsail to steady us and looked back over the breaking surf we'd just come through. Unbelievable is all we could say, but we did it. The LOST SOUL did it, and we were all pretty proud of her, as we set the headsail and made our way into the beating sea to our next anchorage. The seven hour sail to Chinchorro Reef finally brought us all down to reality, and it was almost with a calm demeanor that we passed the reef and motored over the 9- to 10-foot bottom and set our hook behind the reef. We felt we'd seen it all that day. Of course, reality made us take a second look awhile later when we put on our snorkel gear and looked under the boat. It's hard to imaging a 42-ton boat riding just 10 to 12 inches above the sea floor. That's all there was under us for the night we anchored, but by now we just accepted it. We were getting jaded.

The sea gods were not through with us as yet. In order to thoroughly trounce us, they decided to give us a full gale as we were anchored with our silly few inches under us. By morning, we were bouncing on the bottom, again. In three days, my boat'd seen more bottom than a toilet seat!

With a gale blowing we didn't stand a chance in the shallow water we were in, so we decided to make the 102-mile crossing to Cozumel with the gale blowing off our butts. They say sailing downwind is fun, but in over 55,000 miles I haven't seen enough to know. Anyway, we headed carefully out of the anchorage. The water went from eight and a half feet to nine, then to 10, and when it hit 13 we were feeling pretty good. We were doing about five knots idling with the wind pushing us along. No sails up, just the gale pushing us out under bare poles. We were almost out.

Crash! All of a sudden the boat stopped dead in her tracks. No warning, nothing. Just one second the depth sounder said 11 feet, then the next she was buzzing five! Five feet! We had hit a coral head and hit it hard. The boat came to a shuddering halt and people fell all over the decks as they tried to hold themselves up. On the bow, our lookouts were more surprised than I was. They couldn't see the brain coral we'd hit. The 40-knot wind behind us was pushing us up on the coral and the boat heeled to a sickening degree. I slammed it into reverse and gave it full throttle. Slowly, we made a gradual turn and when the wind was on our port side it helped us pull off the rock. With my heart in my throat, we finished finding our way out of the reef.

Once into deep water, Woody jumped overboard. With the seas boiling and the gale blowing he dove down and assessed the damage. A chunk was knocked out of the bottom front of the keel but other than that it looked okay. The rudder was untouched. Woody climbed aboard; we hoisted a double-reefed mainsail and turned toward our destination, some 100 miles off.

It was 8 a.m. Already, we'd had a hell of a day, but it was to get even more exciting. For the next 11½ hours, we set a new record for the LOST SOUL. Over 100 miles. We averaged nine knots for the crossing, and we were in sight of land before sunset. As it got dark we headed for the lee of the island so we could get some rest. We were beat.

Motoryacht *VIRGINIAN*

$\blacktriangleright\!\!\blacktriangleleft$

*A*ll of a sudden, we heard a call on the radio. Motoryacht VIRGINIAN. The 203-foot Feadship VIRGINIAN was in Cozumel. The crew is almost like family since we first met them a few years ago in Nuku Hiva. Then, we ran into them in Papeete, Moorea, Bora Bora. They came into Los Angeles the day we returned home from our South Pacific expedition.

Captain Ingo and his son, Winston, stopped over as soon as we docked. The purser, Bernard, gave us a ride in and we met Rob, Debbie, André, and the rest of the crew for a few beers. This turned into a drinkfest through the night and well into the wee hours of the morning. It was with large heads that we awoke and headed out, trying to beat a storm that was due later in the day.

It almost seems mundane now to tell of our sail up to Isla Mujeres. The most excitement hit just as we passed Punta Cancún. We were hit by one of the biggest fronts I've seen in awhile. All of a sudden, we were trying to feel our way through a reef-studded pass with 50-knot winds blowing first from the south, then the north, and rain coming down so hard you couldn't even see the front of the boat. Top all that off with hellacious lightning and thunder coming down around us, and you get a small idea of what hell must be like.

We made it through, found a place to anchor and settled in at Isla Mujeres. The 25-knot winds that pushed us off anchor were almost anticlimactic, but we finally got our anchor to stick, and John went in to the shrimpers' co-op and liberated two kilos of jumbo shrimp, which were served over cracked ice as we discussed the past three harrowing days. Just three days had seen the poor ol' LOST SOUL hard on the ground, ramming coral heads, breaking records and surfing waves, and surviving one of the biggest fronts she had seen. And to think, we could have been at home watching TV!

Unfortunately, when we got anchored in Isla Mujeres, there was a message waiting at the marina for John and Sue. While we were at sea, John's mother had passed away. They had just one day to get back home, and they hurriedly packed and caught the next plane out. Jody, Woody, Neil, and I sat out the next few days at anchor waiting for the winds to die down and for some new crew who were flying in.

Peter and Willem showed up right on time and, after two days of drinking and thinking, we hoisted anchor and headed out for another leg of our adventure. This time, 290 miles, from the Yucatán Peninsula to Key West, Florida, via the Dry Tortugas.

The first day went pretty much as we have come to expect. Winds on our nose and blowing strong. Right at sunset, we got hit with the mammy of all fronts. This damn thing made the one we hit when we came into Cancún seem like a summer's day. From nowhere, we were hit with winds up to 50 knots from both sides and thunder, lightning and rain in buckets. This lasted for no less than two hours. When it slowed down to 35 knots on our nose this lasted through the evening. The next day was pure heaven as we sailed with 15 knots of wind off our beam and the seas settled in as well. We thought we had it a little too good, and at sunset we found we were right. Another front, just like the one the night before, was there. We turned on our radar and tracked the squalls; we actually managed to steer around them through the night, and made it without a drop of rain, which was weird since we were literally surrounded by squalls. At noon the following day, we arrived at the Dry Tortugas. I'd said as we left Mexico we would arrive at 11:30, and a 30-minute margin for a three day crossing is pretty darned good, if I do say so myself, and I do, since no one else said it!

The Dry Tortugas are made up of three small keys (they call them cays everywhere else, but us Americans have always been weird). On the larger of them is Fort Jefferson, a humongous brick fort built right down to the water's edge. It was built in the 1800s and is the most remote of the national monuments. The anchorage was crowded with fishing boats at night, but during the day we had the place to ourselves, except for all the damned seaplanes that kept landing and taking off around us. I felt like we were anchored in the middle of the runway at Chicago's O'Hare!

The next night, we did an uneventful but very calm motorsail from the Dry Tortugas to Key West, Florida. It was an 80-mile cruise that was done in the most perfect weather we've seen in awhile. On our arrival, we called customs to clear in, and were given a clearance number over the phone.

Key West is a Jimmy Buffett, Ernest Hemingway, gay theme park. Talk about culture shock! Everywhere we went they were playing Jimmy Buffet music, had a photo of Papa Hemingway on the wall, and had an "alternate lifestyle" server. We had a slip with electricity, running water, and cable (which we never even hooked up) and a bar at the end of the dock.

Three days of decadence and relaxation. Well, not exactly relaxation, as we pulled our mainsail to have some repairs done, spent biblical amounts of money at the local West Marine store, and generally cleaned up four months of cruising foreign ports and heavy seas. At the end of the three days, Hippy Pete and Willem boarded a Greyhound for Miami to fly back to Los Angeles, and Woody's lady, Holly, flew in for the trip to Fort Lauderdale. With a lifestyle like this, why on earth would anyone ever want to riot?

I still can't believe it. Jody and I were walking down Duval Street in Key West the day before we were planning to leave, looking for a good place to get an anchovy and garlic pizza (Yeah, they taste better than they smell!). All of a sudden we hear "Hey, Bitchin" from the door of Sloppy Joe's Bar. Out steps Roy Strawn, whom I lived with some 16 years ago in Redondo Beach, and who used to be the director of the American Motorcycle Drag Racing Association. He hauled/dragged/pulled us into Sloppy Joe's, and for the next few hours we relived the past. Now he's the Director of Activities at Sloppy Joe's, the most famous bar in Key West, and he has his own radio show at night. We were forced to drink large quantities of alcoholic beverages and were coerced into dancing, laughing and generally having fun, which, of course, we never do. From now on, I don't think I will ever be surprised where or when I run into anyone!

We barely escaped Key West with our lives, but escape we did. Jody, Woody, Holly, and I made the break and headed out with a beautiful sunset and motored through the night and half the next day, passing Miami Beach and into Fort Lauderdale.

We made our way into the Intracoastal Waterway and spotted the VIRGINIAN right away. We pulled alongside and were soon tied to the dock across from her. We re-made our acquaintances with the captain and crew, and soon settled into one of the biggest spending sprees of the century.

After the five months at sea since we'd left Redondo, we had to re-stock the shelves aboard LOST SOUL. Five trips to the local Costco, a few to West Marine for boat supplies, a couple to McDonald's. Then, we had to get the dinghy motor fixed, buy fuel, and buy more books to read. By the time we were through the week, we had exhausted both the people aboard and the finances.

We left Fort Lauderdale a lot richer than we found it. Restocking after our cruise from California through the canal and the Western Caribbean had us spending money faster than Imelda Marcos at a shoe sale. Soon we were ready to set out once again.

Paradise Is Just a Day Away

———►◄———

A short overnight sail across the channel found us in the beautiful Bahamas. At midday we anchored off Chub Cay to try and check in. We learned how rude folks could be. They want you to pull into the marina to check in and pay them $65 for the privilege of tying up. Our problem was that we draw eight feet, and there was only seven feet, six inches clearance going in. This didn't make a difference to the man doing clearance, who basically told us to go away. We sailed six miles down to a clean anchorage and spent the night. In the morning we opted to sail 17 miles to a small place called Morgan's Bluff on Andros Island. Andros is little visited, but it is the largest island in the Bahamas.

Every place in the Caribbean or Atlantic has a Morgan something. Morgan's Bluff was named for Captain Morgan and it is where he used to hang out when not plundering or raping. The people were friendly, the water was deep and the customs agent only hit us up for a $20 service fee, and he smiled when he got it. We kicked back for awhile and enjoyed our first few days in the Bahamas.

Nassau was a culture shock after sailing the backwoods of Central America for the past five months. Jody and I even made it into one of Merv Griffin's big casinos on Paradise Island and managed to break even, which was a large feat in itself. The pit boss gave us the big eye when we walked in. Obviously, he wasn't used to 300+ pound, tattooed weirdos in cut-off shorts wearing sleeveless T-shirts that say "I hate my boat—it takes my money, but at least it doesn't bitch!" No sense of humor.

We did have some fun playing anchor drill. The bottom in

Nassau Harbor is a shallow layer of sand over hard coral, and the current runs six hours at a time in each direction at four plus knots. The third time we tried to set our hooks we snagged a huge hurricane chain that runs across the bottom of the bay. We had Woody dive down and run a small piece of anchor chain through it, and tie off like a mooring to the hurricane chain. Then we got to sit for the next few days watching frustrated cruisers (like we had been) trying to anchor. But the fun soon wore off, and it was time to bid adieu to our last two guests for awhile. Danny and Mary had sailed with us from Fort Lauderdale, and we hated to see them go. Due to a pair of last minute no-shows, we were left to our own devices for the next month. Just Jody, Woody, and I.

At dawn, we sailed out of Nassau Harbor and headed to a little-known reef crossing area that Ingo, the captain of the VIRGINIAN, told me about. Trusting his latitude and longitude headings, we sailed south of New Providence and soon we were crossing the Great Bahamas Bank in as little as 15 feet of water. We popped our sails and had a very nervous crossing for 36 miles, all the time seeing the bottom as clear as if we were standing on it. Very freaky! Just at sunset we came upon Highborn Cay.

We anchored off a beautiful white sand beach and watched our anchor set in the sand 10 feet below us. The water was so clear you could read CQR on the side of the anchor as it set in the white sand. Just when you think you have finally seen the best, you are forced to find better.

In the morning, according to the weather radio, a front was supposed to come through and the wind would shift to blow us onto the neat white beach. Not wanting to end up as beachcombers, we started checking for a protected anchorage. About five miles south we found it. Hog Cay! Who makes up these names? Nestled between Hog Cay and Wardwick

Cay it was pure paradise. The opening to get inside was about 70 feet wide, but we had plenty of depth.

The whole little anchorage was about 300 feet wide and 1,000 feet long and it was completely surrounded by crystal white sand beaches and the water was clear and smooth as glass. That night the front went through and we slept like babies in a cradle.

Morning came and we explored our paradise. It was three or four little sand cays with palm trees and birds so friendly they would eat out of your hand. We were in the Exumas National Park in the Bahamas. The Exumas run about 200 miles north to south, and are only a few miles wide. The west side is the Great Bahamas Bank, which is only five-thirty feet deep at the deepest and runs up to 30 miles wide. The east side is deep water. We visited the park headquarters and paid $15 for the use of a mooring for two nights.

In the afternoon, the winds shifted to the west, so we took advantage of the weather and sailed out of our little heaven. We sailed through the night, and just before sunset the next evening, we pulled into an anchorage off Crooked Island. We came in just after sunset so we got to set our hook in the dark.

Come dawn, and once again the winds were shifting so we made about 30 miles to the northeast corner of the island, and there we anchored for an evening and waited for a hole in the weather to head out.

Then came *the* day for sailing. We were in awe. At dawn we sailed out off the end of Crooked Island and for the whole day we sailed in the most perfect weather. The wind was strong enough to blow us along at eight knots, but not strong enough to cause high seas. We glided through the crystal clear waters and sailed past Plana Cays and Mayaguana Island, the last two islands in the Bahamas, and then sailed over the top of Caicos. It was great . . . until sunset!

At sunset, the wind shifted to off our nose and upped to over 30 knots. The seas started to build, and by 8 p.m. we were fighting into it once again. I think the sea gods were just teasing us with the great sail that day. First heaven, then hell. We stayed up through the night as the winds increased to a gale and the seas grew to well over 10 feet. At dawn we were about 30 miles out of Grand Turk Island in the Turks and Caicos, making less headway than Dan Quayle at a spelling bee, so we altered course a little to the south and headed in to get out of the weather.

I don't know how I always get into these things, but by the next night Jody, Woody, and I were anchored off Salt Cay, a small paradise south of Grand Turk which has a population of less than 150 people. We found ourselves at a dinner party watching some lady from Egypt do a belly dance in a 150-year-old home!

Turn Left Instead of Right

> ➤◄

I have always thought that a person's life can change unbelievably if, just one morning, he turns left instead of right; figuratively speaking, of course. Thus was this day.

It all started on Grand Turk where Jody and I had stopped for a cold brew at a little place on the beach called Peanuts. We saw a sign that said "Dragon Stout and Rhythm Pills, bring it back." I just had to see what that meant. At the doorway of the little shack an elderly lady named Peanuts, who looked more like Aunt Jemima than anyone on earth, hustled us back through the little kitchen and we found ourselves on a porch on the beach with a picnic table. She told us, in an unbelievable Caribbean accent, to help ourselves to the cold Dragon Stout ale while she made some of her world-famous Rhythm Pills which turned out to be some of the best conch fritters we've ever had.

We met an ex-Wall Street type, now the un-official historian for the Turks and Caicos, who introduced us to a couple of people from Brussels filming a documentary for European television. Little did we know that less than a year later, they would be doing a documentary on us, *Other People's Paradise: Capt. Bob.*

After a few cold ones they took us to the Turks and Caicos Museum, where we met the curator. Then, they invited us to dinner on Salt Cay with Bryan Sheedy, the gentleman who discovered the oldest wreck in the Caribbean (1513).

While at dinner, we met Tom, who works on a cruise ship, and his date, an Egyptian lady who gave belly dance lessons to all the ladies. Jody outdid herself and got the biggest hand from the dozen or so people assembled, but only after partaking in some of the local brew. There was also a couple from Toronto who were there just finishing work on a film for the IMAX screen. I know they will never forget that night, nor will we. A little after midnight we found our way back to the LOST SOUL.

For the next few days we waited out the weather and got to know some very interesting folks. The winds switched around to the north, and we were off again. Three hundred and fifty miles to San Juan, Puerto Rico, where we planned on hauling the boat out to fix the large chunk we took out while bouncing off reefs and things back in Belize.

San Juan is a most interesting place. The first rule is "Do not drive there, because they are crazy drivers!" Jody and I rented a car and drove to the far side of the island to check out a possible haulout. These people stop their cars in the middle of the road, get out and walk into a store to buy something. Meanwhile everyone just sits in their car and waits, or drives up on the sidewalk to get around them. This happened all over the island. Nuts!

After checking the haulout I decided it would be better to try and fix the little chunk in the water, as the hoist was so old it was probably used to hoist the Niña, Pinta, and Santa Maria, when Columbus was in town.

We met a great couple on the boat anchored next to us. Chris was an expatriate Frenchman who used to run night-clubs in New York, and Aleta was from Sausalito. It turned out that Chris was a commercial diver. That evening we downed numerous libations, and with large heads at dawn it was decided he could fix the dent in the bottom while the boat was still in the water. Five hours later, it was done. That night, we did mass quantities of sushi with Chris and Aleta on their boat and prepared for our sail to the Virgin Islands, some 50 miles away.

Came the dawn, and we set off along the north shore of Puerto Rico to a small island called Palomino. It was a picture-perfect place, except it was owned by some hotels and if you weren't a guest you couldn't get a drink there. We decided that we had been thrown out of better places (but not many!), so we went back out to our boat, made cocktails and toasted the sunset, hoping to see a small volcano erupt and blow said island to kingdom-come.

It didn't happen. Anyway, by morning we'd decided to set our sights on the Virgins once again, and we motorsailed to St. Thomas.

At anchor that night our watermaker decided it wanted to stop working. This bummed me out no end, as we had not had to put any water in our tanks since we'd left California. As a matter of fact, as we thought back on it, we hadn't put any water in our tanks since we'd left for the South Pacific, some three years ago.

Oops. I'd forgotten to service the watermaker in the past three years.

A week later, and some $2,000 poorer, we cast off from St. Thomas. I have to admit, we did get a little spoiled as the watermaker was worked on. The marina there had cable TV, and we watched the America's Cup trials each evening, and generally lived the decadent lifestyle. I cannot recommend decadence as a way of life, but it's worked for me!

The annual carnival was held while we were there; steel drum bands, reggae contests, and a general street party every night.

But the real beauty of the Virgin Islands is the outer islands. We sailed over to Jost Van Dyke and anchored in the most picturesque harbor we could imagine. We went to Foxy's and had a couple of piña coladas, and generally acted like tourists, even bought some tourist stuff. When we walked in,

Foxy was playing the guitar and singing, and as he does with most people, he made up a song about the crew from the LOST SOUL.

In the morning we sailed 17 miles to Virgin Gorda. We visited the baths. Unreal! You walk through tunnels cut through granite boulders and stumble into submerged inlets, caves full of water, and just when you think you've seen the best, you come out into Devil's beach.

That night, we picked up a mooring at Coopers Island and had dinner ashore. A great little place tucked under palm trees on a white sand beach. At night it was so clear you could see both the North Star and the Southern Cross. In the morning we motored five miles to Salt Cay where we put on our scuba gear and dove on the wreck of the HMS RHONE, an old steam sailing ship from the 1800s that sank in a storm, and sits in about 50 to 70 feet of water.

After that we went to Norman Cay and explored some caves. One was big enough to dinghy into and inside we found natural bathtubs in the granite walls. The water was so clear looking out the mouth of the cave it looked almost like air, except there were fish swimming in it.

In all we visited six islands in the Virgin Island chain, both U.S. and British. Even though the islands were as beautiful as anyone could ever want, and there were such neat things to see and do, as the baths and diving the RHONE, we still had to head on. It was race week in Antigua, and you know how we love to race. Okay, so we don't love to race, but we do love to party, and rumor has it race week in Antigua is the party of the year for boaters.

We did an overnight 175-mile crossing through a calm sea, and even though we had to motor, it was unbelievable. As we made the straight line from the British Virgin Islands to Antigua, we passed some of the most beautiful places in the world. The sky was like dark blue velvet with diamonds in it, and the islands' lights looked like piles of jewels sparkling in the evening.

Anguilla, Saba (looks like a volcano going 3000 feet straight up!), St Kitts, Nevis, and Montserrat passed off our bows. At dawn, we spotted Antigua. As we approached the island, we saw over 200 sailboats under full sail coming out to greet us. Okay, not to greet us. Actually, it was the first of the big races, but we can dream, can't we?

As the 200 boats from England, Spain, France, the U.S., Japan and Australia jockeyed for position, we slipped into English Harbour and took a spot to anchor. As the race ended we were surrounded with boats. You could almost walk to shore from boat to boat, they were anchored so close. My favorite entry was the one from the Virgin Islands. This guy's whole crew were gorgeous ladies, topless. They were a very popular entry.

After a week of fixing and relaxing we were ready for another little crossing.

Another Short Cut

---◄►---

*O*nce again, it was time to set sail for far flung places. We waited about a week after most boats left when race week was over. Actually we were waiting for a few parts for our generator, and then it was time to head out into the great void.

For this leg we had 26-year-old Woody Henderson, who'd been with us since we left Southern California, and Canadian Luke Rosenau, who had sailed with us from Papeete to Hawaii a year earlier. Luke had decided he needed a little more adventure in his 19-year-old life.

We sailed up to St. John's Harbour on the north end of Antigua to provision, and in the morning took off for our last stop, the island of Barbuda. Barbuda is a small desert island with an 11-mile uninterrupted white sand beach, and very few people. This was to be our jumping off point to cross the Atlantic.

I have to admit I had some misgivings about our route. Our plan was to sail our own route, ignoring the sailing directions touted by most of the sailing folk. All the other boats leaving for Europe from Antigua race week sailed 600 miles north to Bermuda, and then planned to get a boost from the westerlies, up around 40 degrees.

Now, this plan is similar to what most folks do sailing from Hawaii to the U.S. mainland, and for the same reasons. You get north to where it blows, and then head across with a tailwind. Only problem with that is, it's cold up there! I hate the cold! Not only that, my boat sails like a drunken sailor on a direct downwind run. It slogs back and forth, and is about as much fun as riding a camel with a hangover. And so it was that we set sail directly for the Azores from the little island of Barbuda.

•-•

Some five days and 750 miles later we were under spin-naker as we drifted in the warm southern climes, on a direct B-line to the Azores. The first week was as ideal as a crossing could be. We sailed with a beam wind for most of the time, and then it switched off our stern. Each night we enjoyed gourmet meals fixed by Jody and Luke, and during the day we kicked back and cruised. About the fifth night out we en-countered some clouds, and a few times we got a free boat wash, as they would dump mass quantities of warm rainwater on the boat, but the sun would dry it almost as fast as we got wet.

Nine hundred miles out of Barbuda we hooked up with a 120-pound white marlin. They aren't very good to eat so we released him. We didn't have enough room in the freezer if we'd wanted to keep him, so it was just as well.

A little before six a.m., on the seventh day of the crossing, I woke up to feel the hull plastered against my left cheek. I made my way to the cockpit by walking on bulkheads and found we were, indeed, laying on our starboard side. A less-than-enjoyable way to awaken to a new day.

Luke was on watch and he said the winds were being "a little funny." I looked around. We were surrounded by dark clouds, and one particularly bad group had lightning flashing all around and was darker than Stephen King's humor.

We were being sucked into the squall from hell. We were backwinded by a 50- to 60-mile an hour gust, snapping the mainsail preventer like Schwarzenegger snaps a geek's neck, backwinding the headsail and making the prevented mizzen sail look like a pretzel. Jody and Woody made it into the cock-pit as we laid at a sickening angle, knocked down in the water.

Now this is the third time in some 50,000 miles I've had this happen and I don't like it at all. The LOST SOUL was just laying on her side with the sail in the water and the deck on a

60-degree tilt. It only lasted a few seconds until we could loosen the head sheet and mainsail, but those seconds seemed like an eternity while sitting on our side, literally one-half of the way across the Atlantic Ocean. We were 1,050 miles from Antigua and 1,230 miles from the Azores.

We got the sails pulled down and the squall abated to 25-35 knots, and we assessed the damage. We'd pulled an eye out of the mainsail boom, ripped open our headsail that we'd just fixed the day before, and lost a cover for our scuba tanks on the foredeck. Other than that we had a bunch of crap all over the saloon and other cabins, and a fire extinguisher broke loose and flew across the cabin breaking the frame that held the radio licenses for the boat. It took a while to straighten it all up. Meanwhile, we put up the storm canvas and got to play hide and seek with rain for the rest of the day.

Then the electrical gods started to play with us. One night the knotmeter decided it wanted to take some time off, so it started to go haywire. All of a sudden we didn't know how fast we were going, but we still had our handy-dandy GPS to tell us that. The next night the GPS died. The GPS tells us little things like where we are, how far we have to go, and in what direction. You know, the little things in life, that, all of a sudden, seem so important 1,000 miles from nowhere. Of course, us dummies on the LOST SOUL, which we started to call the *Really Lost Soul*, have great backups. So after five hours of playing let's try to fix the GPS, we decided to go for door number two, and fire up our backup, handheld GPS. A half hour later we discover it wasn't getting satellite readings.

But we aren't through playing backup yet. We have an 11-year-old Magnavox SatNav stashed on the boat. We get it all on line, only to realize we have to put in an approximate position to make it acquire a satellite when one passes by, and the last fix this antique had was when Magellan radioed Cortez for a position.

So here we were, midway across the Atlantic Ocean, in a multi-gross megabuck yacht with all the latest electronic equipment and three backups, and we didn't know where in hell we were.

For awhile I went through the ship's log from the previous day and came up with a dead-reckoning position, fed it into the SatNav, and voilà! In a few minutes it was spitting out latitude and longitude. Of course, we still had our trusty sextant on board, but the last time I used it was crossing from Mexico to Hawaii some 18 years ago, and I might have been a little rusty.

About 13 days into the crossing we were 350 miles out of the Azores and had been becalmed for about a week. That means we motored day and night. That's about as much fun as having Mike Tyson as a cellmate tell you he's gay. Aside from the wear and tear on the engine, it eats a lot of fuel. So here we were, still 300 miles out, and our fuel was getting as scarce as morals in Congress. Marvelous!

When we figured we were almost out of fuel we lowered the rpms on the engine and tried to get every last minute of fuel from the tank. We keep 20 gallons for emergencies in plastic jugs in our deck-box, but those are saved for running the generator and emergency maneuvering, if we run out. At three in the morning, while Woody was on watch, we were cruising through a dead calm, and we were sure we would start spluttering any minute. We had actually gone 16 hours longer than we had expected. Then a small breeze hit us. Then it got stronger, and by four a.m. we were sailing and shut off the engine, Before we'd run out of fuel!

The wind blew up to 20 knots and soon we were in sight of Horta, on the island of Faial, in the Azores. We had planned on going to São Miguel, but Horta was closer, so at the last minute our plans were changed.

As we pulled into the little bay at Horta, we had to wait for a boat to pull away from the customs dock so we could clear in. As we turned into the bay we saw it was a very large motoryacht. As we got closer we saw it was none other than the VIRGINIAN. We see more of these guys than we do our parents!

Decadence? You Bet!

>———————————◄

*A*fter our clearance we side tied to the 203-foot VIRGIN-
IAN, as the harbor was full and there was no place else
to tie-up. For the next week we lived in the lap of luxury. The
crew of the large luxury yacht plugged us into their electricity,
filled our tank with water (they made 5,000 gallons a day!), gave
us our own laundry room (they have eight on board!) and even
gave us some fuel (they carry 65,000 gallons, who's gonna miss
a lousy 300-400?). They also gave us free run of the jacuzzi.

The VIRGINIAN's crew hung out on the LOST SOUL while in
port. They said it was more comfortable. Kewl!

When we painted the name of the LOST SOUL on the dock
next to where they painted their name, they wrote "Tender to
the VIRGINIAN" under the LOST SOUL's name. Not to be outdone,
we wrote "Supply ship to LOST SOUL" under their name.

While at the customs dock we ran into a guy who had just
been with Janet and Samantha, our old crew from Hawaii,
while they were in Aspen, Colorado, just a couple of weeks
earlier. He'd seen a photo of me and the girls, and recognized
me. Let's see, a guy from New York crewing on a boat from the
Med was with two girls in Aspen who crewed on a yacht from
California while in Hawaii and meets that boat in the Azores.
Why not?

In any case, once we got over old home week with Ingo,
Rob, Debbie, André, Dana, John, Mike, and the crew of the
VIRGINIAN, we started to explore Horta.

What a great place. A small island in the middle of the
Atlantic Ocean with rolling green hills, a town of the friend-
liest people on earth and a true crossroads of the world for the
past 500 years. Columbus stopped here on the way back from

discovering some place to the west. It had been a shipping and whaling center back then. Whaling stopped there about 30 years ago, but they kept the whales' teeth and bones, and it is one of the few places where you can still get true scrimshaw, which is intricate carvings on whale teeth.

In order to maintain the image of the LOST SOUL, we had a little party on board. We were still side tied to the Virginian, and after a few hours of downing mass quantities of sushi and spicy tuna rolls, we started to get a little drunk. Jody and I ended up in the jacuzzi, being totally decadent. Meanwhile Luke and Woody went out to do a little partying in town, at about midnight.

The next day we found Woody in blood-covered sheets, and suffering from a hangover of biblical proportions. We went to the crew of the VIRGINIAN and then the story unfurled. It seems that they started a little after midnight. They found a couple of girl scouts who had some wine. Seems the drinking age is 15 in Portugal. Anyway, after they drank the girl scouts' wine, they found a Portuguese with a bottle of local white. They downed that, and shortly thereafter it seems Woody had completely lost his mind.

John, from the VIRGINIAN, tried to take care of him but Woody wouldn't have anything to do with it. He said he was fine, jerked away from John, and started bumping his way down the narrow streets of Horta. Then he went down, hard, and split his head against a concrete bench and was out like a light. John and a local tried to help him, but they couldn't carry him, so they went to the boat for help. Meanwhile, another local found him lying there, along with a couple of guys from the VIRGINIAN, who didn't even know it was Woody (they were a bit soused themselves). All of this was going on at about five in the morning.

So anyway, the dawn comes with half the harbor pissed

off because of all the noise, the VIRGINIAN crew ready to lynch Woody for keeping them awake, and Woody passed out with a large head gash and bloody sheets. Ah, wasted youth.

I, of course, being an old fart, slept through it all, and didn't even know anything was wrong until well into the afternoon, when some of the participants filled me in.

Of course, not to be outdone, the crew of the VIRGINIAN had to cause a ruckus. This was done in the form of Debbie, the crew's cook, trying to ride her Harley-Davidson: yeah, the damned boat is so big they have two Harleys, a Kawasaki, three speed boats and two sailboats on board! I say "trying" to ride her Harley, because in three days she managed to dump it twice.

It was time to take off. One of the VIRGINIAN's deck crew, a lady named Frances, signed on to sail to Porto Velas with us. We made arrangements to meet with VIRGINIAN there, and some four hours later, after a great sail, we were rafted up to the dock in this small Azores port. They had never seen a boat as large as the VIRGINIAN, and the whole town came out to check her out. Unfortunately, the surge was pretty strong, and after a couple of hours we had to cast off. As we headed south we were passed by VIRGINIAN as she headed off to Glascow, Scotland. This was the last we'd see of her and her crew. A little while later her owner passed away, and she was sold.

We went through the night, and by morning the winds were right off our noses. We headed to a small bay called Porto Silvera on the island of Terceira. There we sat for a few days waiting for the weather to turn around like it's supposed to, and blow us the 1,100 miles we still had to go to get to Gibraltar.

We tired of waiting after three days, and decided to go for it. We talked to TICONDEROGA, a very famous and beautiful 1936 ketch, on the sideband radio, and we both decided to head out the next morning. They were leaving from Horta, about 60 miles behind us. In the morning we both took off.

The same morning we talked with another boat, BIG O, out of Sausalito. It was owned by Richard Spindler, who publishes *Latitude 38*. We'd been playing tag with them ever since sailing down the Baja peninsula some seven months earlier. They were about 200 miles in front of us. As the truckers would say, we were in the "rocking chair." We were trying to get up over the high that was causing easterly winds, so we headed slightly north, up to about 40 degrees, and then leveled off. The first night out, we got a little surprise.

One minute we're motoring along in a 13-knot breeze, then for a second our staysail backs, then wham! We were hit right in the ass with a waterspout. The mast slaps the water harder than Zsa-Zsa smacks a Beverly Hills cop. All of a sudden we're all lying with our faces against a bulkhead wondering what the hell hit us. Fortunately, there was no damage, and in a matter of minutes our hearts started to beat a normal beat, and we went back about our business. For the next three days we fought winds up to 35 knots, and beat into seas that make the North Atlantic such an unpopular cruising ground.

It was here that we found we had lost a friend in the storm. Jody walked forward during a lull in the winds to say hello to Dolly, our full-sized wooden dolphin figure head we'd had carved in Hawaii. A few minutes later she returned to the cockpit with tears in her eyes. It seems that during the night, the dolphins had broken her loose, and she was now swimming in the Atlantic, telling the local dolphins of her harrowing days as a figurehead all the way from Hawaii, through the Panama Canal, and here to the North Atlantic. There was a real feeling of loss aboard the LOST SOUL.

But life goes on. A couple of times a day we'd talk with

TICONDEROGA on the sideband radio, comparing weather notes. They started 60 miles behind us, and halfway across we were still within a few miles of each other. At last the winds subsided some 450 miles out of Gibraltar, and we got some well-earned rest. Both boats came through like troopers, as did the crews.

Sunset on the thirtieth day of the Atlantic crossing. Just one week after leaving the Azores, we sighted Europe. That night we made our way into a large channel. At dawn we were off Portugal, then Spain came into view with Morocco on the other side. Algiers radio fought with Cádiz for air time as we motored toward the fabled Straits of Gibraltar. We listened to radio calls in Arabic, Spanish, Portuguese, French, Greek, Italian and English. Not real American English, but that other stuff, with a bunch of "rather" and "bloody hells." We entered the Straits about nine miles behind TICONDEROGA, and as we squeezed through the tight entrance to the Med we watched literally hundreds of ships crisscrossing as they hauled their cargos to Europe, the Far East, and the New World.

I admit it, I was impressed. Here we were entering the fabled Mediterranean. Nothing in 20 years of cruising had prepared me for the feeling of accomplishment that filled me. We had done it. From Southern California, through the Panama Canal, across the Caribbean and the Atlantic, and into "Rome's Lake." I had read about it in history books since I was first able to read, and here we were.

The Med at Last

———————►◄———————

*O*ur arrival in Gibraltar started a whole new cruising experience. When you cruise it seems that you break the cruise up, at least in your mind, into sections. We'd had the Mexico experience, we'd sailed the South Pacific scene, Hawaii was an adventure of its own, and then there was the Caribbean, and finally the Atlantic crossing. We were now about to set off on our Mediterranean adventure.

I have to admit, I looked forward to this leg with more anticipation than a groom on his wedding night. I was a little giddy at the thought of what was finally about to happen, but also afraid that it might not be all that it's supposed to be.

Our crew, consisting of Woody Henderson, Luke Rosenau, Captain Bob and Admiral Jody landed in Gibraltar and spent three days playing with the apes (yeah, they run wild on the top of the rock!). We checked out some giant caves, tried miscellaneous ales, ciders and brews at the pubs and generally had a tourist kind of time. The first Sunday we spent aboard the ketch TICONDEROGA at a party. TICONDEROGA is about the most perfect wooden boat I have ever seen, having undergone a recent $1.5 million refit. As we walked her decks with Captain Tom I couldn't believe how perfect a boat could be.

Then we looked up and saw what has to be the most beautiful schooner I've ever seen pulling around the corner. She pulled in next to us and I was in love again. The 1930s schooner ALTAIR is about 100 feet and maintained to perfection. They had just finished her refit, for $2.5 million. The party soon moved aboard ALTAIR and the rest of the day was spent feeling a little like a, uh, hooker in church?

A few days later we fueled up at the dock at the Queen's Quay in Gibraltar, and we headed out into the Med. We spent our first day sailing downwind off the coast of Spain. By dawn the next morning we had passed Cabo de Gata and swung to the northeast heading toward the Balearic Islands. Our first port was at Ibiza, Spain.

Ibiza may be a little behind the times, but they have taken disco and refined it to a pure science. These folks are just plain weird. John Travolta could be elected God here, and Michael Jackson would be a saint! First of all, the sun doesn't go down until after 9:30 p.m. Then it starts. At about 11:30 p.m. the discos start to open. Some don't even open until 6 a.m. The people come from all over Europe to disco, and they do it all night long. It is normal to sit at a sidewalk cafe, there are more sidewalk cafes than notches on Madonna's headboard. It is also a great place to see people from Italy, Germany, England, Greece, France and who knows where else. If you eavesdrop at these places it sounds like you are at the Tower of Babel.

The way it works is this. You hit the first disco at about 11:30 p.m. and at 2 a.m. it closes, and another one opens up down the street. The whole crowd heads over there, in a pack. At around 5 a.m. that one closes, and another opens elsewhere. Once again the exodus takes place. My poor misbegotten crew came stumbling home at 9 a.m. more than once.

Wonder why they didn't feel like varnishing?

Of course I, being an old grump, decided I'd rather see the days than the nights, so I abstained from said foolishness.

It was about time for Father's Day, and my dad had been in the hospital, so I figured this would be a good time to fly back home for a few days. Besides, a good friend needed me to give a deposition, and his lawyers agreed to pay for my ticket home, first class! Couldn't pass that up, could I?

Jet lag, what a concept! After eight months of leisure sailing the 10,000 miles from home to Ibiza, I made the return flight in 20 hours. They seemed one hell of a lot longer than the eight months. I guess that goes to prove the old adage, "The difference between ordeal and adventure is attitude."

After all, leaving my boat in paradise and flying home, let's just say my attitude was somewhere between that of an ax murderer and a raving psychotic.

The four days passed faster than a first date with Julia Roberts. I was seeing everyone I could at home and spending 10 hours locked up with a bunch of lawyers, giving a deposition for a friend. The 24-hour return flight knocked me on my rather large butt, and I spent the first couple of days back on the boat with walking pneumonia. A storm came in and kicked us around at our slip so we had to go out to sea, and our electrical system went zap.

But in all, it was better being there than being back home. While I'd been back in Redondo Beach, I'd had a mechanic working on an engine problem we'd started having on our way from Gibraltar to Ibiza. We'd put in two gallons of oil, and four hours later we'd take out four gallons. About $1,300 later, he said it was fixed. He lied! He also worked on the generator. The first of many to do this.

Ah, but I'm always one to look for a silver lining. From here I had nowhere to go but up. Soon the winds abated, we pulled back into a slip for a day, re-wired our wayward electrical problems, and Woody's girlfriend Holly flew in. She'd brighten anyone's attitude. Life was looking good again, and we departed Ibiza and headed across the 60 miles to Palma de Mallorca.

The old days are over. Remember when sailing men went to the sea in ships? The Saturday Night Live crew knew how it was, with John Belushi, Chevy Chase and the guys doing

manly things on the HMS RAGING QUEEN. Well, things had de-
generated here on the LOST SOUL. I came topside to find Woody
and Luke fighting, or should I say whining, over who would
get the latest issue of *Cosmopolitan* that Holly brought so they
could do the quiz. You know, "Is your lover a fag?" or "How
does your sexuality rate?" or "Are you a modern woman?" A
few days at sea, after *Cosmopolitan* had magically "disappeared" (so I'm guilty!) and *Easyrider* had taken its rightful
place on the table, things got back to normal.

We sailed out of Palma and made it about 30 miles to a
small anchorage near Puerto Petro on the south side of Mallorca. We anchored for the night, surrounded by caves, high
sandstone cliffs, and clear blue water. For the first time in the
Med we went swimming off the boat, as the water temperature
was into the mid-70s. Still a little less than what we'd become
accustomed to in the Caribbean and South Pacific, but livable.

During the night a small mistral, a north wind, blew up
and the anchorage became lumpier than last night's mashed
potatoes, so at dawn we hoisted anchor and motored up to a
protected bay. We spent the day at anchor enjoying the warm
sun and walking through the quaint little town, and at dawn
headed out for Menorca, the smaller of the Spanish Balearic
Islands. We anchored in Fornells on the north coast of
Menorca. This place was first settled by the Phoenicians 1600
B.C. Some of the original buildings still stand more than 3500
years later.

Once again, at dawn, much to the chagrin of my crew, we
headed out for the 230-mile sail from Menorca to the southern
coast of France. We had a special breakfast of sourdough pan-
cakes and fresh homemade bread to help Woody celebrate his
birthday. Twenty six! I've got underwear older than that. That
night at sea we had roast beef, baked potatoes, asparagus and
birthday cake.

Adventures in Frog Land

*A*nd then began the adventures of the LOST SOUL in Frog Land (with apologies to those of frog extraction). First of all let's talk about great disappointments, like arriving in Saint Tropez, and finding a grubby little marina with prices that would scare the hell out of Howard Hughes' ghost. We spent one night, and then headed out for Cannes. We still had the same problem we had before, with the engine oil getting thin and doubling, so we had to look for another mechanic, this time in France. The mechanic charged us 2,000 francs to change a lift pump (about $500). He also worked on the generator, but to no avail.

At least Cannes had some social redeeming aspects. You can't believe how many topless ladies there were on the beach! Of course half of them should have been paid to put their suits back on, but the other half more than made up for it. Jody was well occupied watching the young dudes. They wear bikinis too.

And then there is shopping in a country where we don't speak the language, or just try getting along in general. What fun. Like talking to the customs guy. He spoke no English, I spoke no French, so we conversed in Spanish, and got along great.

At the meat market with our friend from Algiers, we had full blown comedy at its best. Jody and I stood and asked what type of meat a certain cut was by raising our shoulders with hands in the air; he would either "bleat" like a sheep, "moo" like a cow, "snort" like a pig or "gobble" like a turkey. We got some great moo, a little snort and some bleat for later.

While we were in port a U.S. Navy warship came in and landed a bunch of troops with shore leave. It felt good seeing people dress and talk like back home. We did a once around their ship with our loudspeakers blaring "Stars and Stripes Forever" and Jody actually got tears in her eyes. Must have been dust in the air or something.

They held the Cannes Jazz Festival the same week we were there, in an amphitheater just a few hundred yards from where we anchored, so each night we got a free concert. I can honestly say the trip to the Med became a worthwhile endeavor.

After a week we headed over to Nice and anchored off the airport. On Friday night my friend Danny flew in from California, the next day Woody's girlfriend Holly flew out, and the following day Jody's girlfriend Dianne flew in from Salt Lake City. Once again we had a full crew and we headed over to anchor in Villefranche-sur-Mer, about five miles from Monaco.

As we sat sipping a cool Heineken at a sidewalk cafe on the quay I happened to look up at a flag flying on a pole out front. It seems that Villefranche was having an anniversary. Their 700th anniversary. The town was founded in 1295. 1295! Back home we put up a plaque if a building is older than the earthquake of 1968!

I must digress for a moment. It seems that when I was born, my mother had a best friend who went to the University of Southern California with her. That friend got married about the same time as my mother, had a son around the time my older brother was born, another son when I was born, and a daughter about the time my sister was born. We six children were raised together until 1959, when I was 15 years old. At that time, the son who was my age, my best friend Ronnie Patterson, went astray. You see, he was a violin prodigy, and he went off to play the fiddle with some guy named Jascha Heifetz. I, of course, turned in the correct direction, and went off to ride motorcycles and raise hell.

Anyway, here we are 35 years later, and I find that my childhood friend Ronnie is still leading his miscreant lifestyle. For the past decade or so, he has been the Concert Master at the Monaco Philharmonic Orchestra, and we are anchored just five miles away! We spent the next couple of days lying to each other about our lives. He took us on a tour of Prince Rainier's Palace. He got a couple of points on me there; he's a personal friend of Rainier and Prince Albert! We then went over to Princess Grace's gravesite, he played solo at her funeral and was a close friend of hers. Then we went to his house on the hillside overlooking the Med that he built himself. I met his wife and three kids and listened to some of the albums they'd done in the past couple decades. I guess with some people there is no playing "Top this!" Made my life as a bike bum and sailor seem more than a little drab. By the time we bid each other adieu it seemed like the 35 years had never happened. It was tough to leave.

We did an overnighter across to the island of Corsica, making landfall early the next day at Calvi. Once again we were humbled as we walked through the citadel that was built on the site where the Romans landed in 228 B.C. We walked the ancient streets that wound through the city and acted like tourists.

Meanwhile we found a mechanic again, this time one who spoke absolutely no English, and let him try to fix again our oil problem. At this point we had spent a little over $2,000, and still had the same problem. He fiddled with the generator also.

As it was July 14, Bastille Day, we had to hang out in Calvi while he rebuilt our fuel system.

Actually it was not too bad a deal hanging out there. One day we took a train along the coast of Corsica, and the rest of the time we just enjoyed the scenery. Danny got eyestrain, and still has black and blue marks where the binoculars were jammed in his face for four days watching the gorgeous ladies on the boats anchored around us.

After the holiday was over Jean Paul Magot (really, that's his name!) returned and installed the re-built injector pump and the injectors, and we fired it up. It seemed to work and I paid him the 3,500 francs (about $800) he asked. That put me almost to $3,000 trying to find the problem in Spain, mainland France and Corsica. Only time would tell if it worked. The engine ran fine after that, but the generator was still acting up.

We motored 40 miles south to a small anchorage in Ajaccio Bay, and spent the night anchored under a medieval keep that was part of the lookout system they had some 1000 years ago. The next day we headed into what would be one of the best stops of our Mediterranean trip so far, Bonifacio. This place almost defies description, but I have to give it a shot.

First of all finding the entrance to this harbor was harder than to find a teenager's motives. It is in a sheer cliff, with 100-foot high caves on each side of the entrance. One cave reminded me of the fabled Blue Grotto, and we took our dinghy way inside, where you could get out of the dinghy on ledges and walk around deep inside the cave, the only light coming from the blue reflection of the clear waters. The whole coast consisted of bleached white sheer cliffs that went up hundreds of feet, and there, perched on top was the fabled citadel of Bonifacio. Built almost 1000 years ago, this fortress sits on top of the cliffs looking straight down 500-600 feet. On the other side of the citadel there is a harbor, and the only entrance is a couple of hundred feet wide, and then it opens up and goes back almost a mile.

It was here that we discovered our generator had quit working. The old adage that cruising is fixing your boat in new and exotic places is really true. It looked like our engine problem was solved, and now our generator was going in the crapper.

That afternoon we were told that all of the injectors were bad. Each was $150, another $100 to get them shipped from the States, and they wouldn't be here for a week, which means we had them shipped to the Isle of Capri, where we should be by then. But first the engine-driven refrigeration had to go out. With no generator the only way to keep our stuff cold was with the engine-driven compressor. Naturally it took a poop that afternoon.

So I put on our backup, and it worked, for two hours. Then the freon was all gone from the system.

But the world goes on. We sailed across the straits of Bonifacio to a place called Little Tahiti, just 5 miles from Porto Cervo. I ran a new refer line, vacuumed and recharged the system, and found out that my backup Honda generator took a poop.

In the meantime here was this little octopus, minding its own business, and along swim Jody and Dianne. It is still up in the air as to who was more disturbed, the girls or the octopus, but they all went their separate ways, squirting various bodily fluids. The screams echoed for miles.

And then Jody got the crabs! You see, she kept finding pretty seashells, and since she had no place where to put them, she stuck them in her bikini bottoms. After all, it was a topless area, and when in Rome. . . . One had a hermit crab in it. Suffice it to say, the hermit crab found a warm and snugly new home, and in its haste to relocate, it decided to bite Jody on a very tender portion of her anatomy. Let me put it this way, we won't be showing slides of this bite at the next seminar.

Little Tahiti was well named. There were two small white sand beaches, crystal clear, bright blue waters, a couple of palm trees and about a million of Riva speed boats from over Porto Cervo, just 5 miles away.

A little oddity. It seems that American yachts in that area are as scarce as virgins in a maternity ward. In the month we sailed the waters of Spain, France and Italy we did not see one other boat from America. Not one, unless you count the Navy warship anchored in Cannes.

We sailed to Porto Cervo, which had been touted as the finest marina in the world, built by the Aga Khan and a few of his billionaire buddies, but when we got there it was just another Med-style concrete marina. You anchor and back to a concrete quay. There were a lot of big boats, but other than that I find the marinas back home superior.

We just turned around and headed out, and sailed a few miles farther south to a clean beach. Danny took his place on the aft deck with the binoculars as we anchored and enjoyed the sunshine and view.

Late in the afternoon a wind blew in, and we saw a 150-foot Parini Navi with red, white and blue flying, out there setting her sails. Not to be outdone, we hoisted anchor and hauled up the sails on the LOST SOUL. When we got out into the windline it was blowing at about 25 knots, so we pulled alongside the XASTRIA and popped all our sails, only to find that the flag she flew was Liberian, which is similar to the American flag, but with only one star. What a kick sailing at 9 to10 knots next to a 20-million-dollar megayacht and keeping up. Soon they furled their sail by pressing buttons, and pulled into an anchorage.

It was then that we found the anchorage of the really rich and famous. There were at least 10 boats anchored that were over 150 feet and one, the ALEXANDER, was well over 300 feet. It looked like a cruise ship.

We pulled into a marina that was so small Mickey Rooney

couldn't turn around in it, and bought 60 gallons of fuel to get us to the mainland of Italy. It was just under $4 per gallon, and at that price pretty spendy, but less than the almost five dollars per gallon they wanted in France. We anchored off another great beach and spent the day watching beachgoers and the night watching *Scarface* on video. We had to practice our Italian, didn't we? After an overnight stop in a small anchorage in Sardinia, we headed out for the most famous island in the Mediterranean, Capri.

The Isle of Capri

➤◄

*C*apri was everything we expected. The waters were deep blue, the people friendly, and the only problem was the damned Blue Grotto. They charge $10 a head to go into the grotto, but you have to go in their little wooden dugout boats. The catch is that they won't take you in their little wooden dugout boats unless you are on a tour ship or a land tour. So we got to sit outside looking in, and we couldn't even hire a boat to take us inside. Of course Woody and Luke weren't to be deterred so easily, and they squeezed into the grotto in the inflatable (slightly deflated to make it fit) just after "closing time."

At the top of the island, the city of Anacapri sits astride a 3000-foot peak and looks straight down on the bay. Absolutely beautiful.

We didn't get to enjoy the beauty long, however, as our generator had been quits for two weeks since Corsica, and we were waiting for parts to come in. We had arranged for them to be shipped to a small cafe on the island. After a week they arrived. The damn things cost $500 and the problem wasn't fixed. With some searching we heard we could find a mechanic over on the mainland, so we headed the 16 miles across the bay to a small town called Baia, and there we found not only a mechanic, but the nicest town we had stayed in the whole trip. This place was the Mayberry RFD of Italy.

No, it wasn't the most beautiful. Just the best. It is on the mainland of Italy about 10 miles from Naples. This little spot, a small protected natural harbor, is where Nero, one of the most powerful emperors of Rome, killed his mother. This is where the pervert Caligula lived, and just a couple of miles from where Brutus and Mark Anthony hatched the plans to murder Caesar. It was the sight of the largest Roman resort on the Med.

We were the only cruising boat there, and the only tourists. The people watching was superb. In the evening, on the square in front of the train station, you would find practically the whole town, sitting around talking, or having a beer or gelato (ice cream) at a small place called "The Monkey Bar." Each night the town would gather there. The older folks sat on benches sipping tea, while the youngsters walked around the parking lot, discussing the new motorscooters and cars. The middle-aged folks sat at small tables, sipping wine. The LOST SOUL crew made a big hit. Even though we spoke no Italian, a little bit of Spanish seemed to go a long way, and the town adopted us as we waited for parts.

One day, we went to the city of Pompeii, which was buried in the year 79 by an explosion of Mt. Vesuvius. The town was preserved for almost 2000 years under the ashes. It was amazing to walk those streets after all that time, and see the city exactly as it was.

Our generator was soon running again and we headed out on the next leg of our adventure. First we had to stop back in Capri to say goodbye to the friends we'd made at a small cafe there. The family had taken us in as we waited for the parts and we had some great evenings. I don't think I will ever forget arm-wrestling half the town one night at their outdoor cafe. I can't remember ever feeling so at home.

But once again the adventure gods called, and we were off, heading south towards the Straits of Messina. The first night we were hit by all the bad weather we'd missed so far. Thunderheads, lightning, rain and winds blew us to the Island of Stromboli. This place should be called "the land that time forgot." It is a sheer-sided active volcano sticking up about

2,700 feet into the sky. It is known as the world's oldest lighthouse. There is a river of molten lava flowing down the side, and a cloud of smoke belching out the top, to lead sailors to the Straits of Messina.

Odyssey, Here We Come

*I*t was Stromboli that Ulysses used as a guide to find the straits in the Odyssey. Fifty miles farther south and we entered the Straits of Messina.

Just like Ulysses we found the whirlpool, only methinks the dude exaggerated just a tad. We got caught in one and all it did was pull us around a little. We also passed the spot where the sirens called to him on his ship, but we didn't hear nothing but an out-of-tune tenor on the beach wearing a G-string.

That evening we anchored off a beach called Villa di Calabria, and it was a most pleasant last stop in Italy. A resort town for the middle class, it consisted of a great beach and a bunch of what looked like dressing rooms, but in actuality were little 6 by 10 rooms with a bed and bath in them. We supped on the best pizza we'd had in Italy, and at dawn we hoisted the iron again and headed out of the straits into the Ionian Sea, still on the path of Ulysses. We sailed out from under the toe of the boot, made a b-line for the heel and enjoyed a very relaxed sail.

The 230-mile crossing of the Ionian Sea was one of the best sails we'd had, and at six that evening we were entering Argostoli, Cephalonia in Greece.

Of course first we needed our little touch of excitement. We were sailing with a 25-knot aft wind, doing about 9 to 10 knots. Woody was at the wheel as the autopilot couldn't handle the trailing seas. All of a sudden Woody turned around, looked at me, and started spinning the steering wheel.

Are steering wheels supposed to do that? Uh, I don't think so. The steering didn't work!

Now, being in a 42-ton sailboat barreling downwind at 10 knots toward a large rock with no steering can make you nervous, and we were. We soon had the problem under control as Woody steered the boat from the inside steering station and the rest of us Mickey Moused the upper steering station to get us in. We pulled up to the dock in Argostoli and breathed a very large sigh. We were in Greece!

We had reached the mid-point of our voyage, and this was what we'd sailed some 12,000 miles to see. It turned out to be well worth the trip. Greece has some of the best cruising grounds we have yet to come across. Our arrival in Greece was on the island of Cephalonia on the western end of the Gulfs of Corinth and Poros. If there is one thing that stands out about Greece, besides the great weather, nice anchorages, pretty women and friendly people, it is the food. Jody and I were like two kids in a candy store. Every day we had a Greek salad. We wolfed down lamb and veal fixed more ways than Zsa-Zsa had husbands. We stuffed ourselves with dolma (stuffed grape leaves), tzaziki (a yogurt cucumber blend to die for) and souvlaki (skewered lamb, pork and beef). Greece has more specialties than Heidi Fleiss!

After Cephalonia our stay in Vathi, on the island of Ithaca, was idyllic. Plenty of great tavernas and shops to stroll through and a quiet anchorage. We motored from there five miles up the coast to a small sandy beach, and there met the 93-foot schooner YAAR, out of Gibraltar. We had been sailing with them for about five days up the islands. Early that afternoon the winds came up and we bid adieu to the crew of YAAR and caught the north wind for a great sail 20 miles across the channel to a very small uninhabited island called Oxia. It looked just like an Alpine lake. Deep crystal blue waters and sheer white cliffs with dark green growth, and not one other person on the whole island! We expected a buxom maid to come strolling down a hill singing the *Sound of Music*.

The next day we found paradise of another kind. We sailed into the Gulf of Corinth and set our hook at Nafpaktos, a town older than a Milton Berle joke. This is the most perfectly preserved medieval harbor in the Med. As you pull up in the anchorage you are looking through the entrance of a gate into a small man-made harbor surrounded by castle walls, and the walls wind their way 4000 feet up the mountainside to a castle. There is a square just above the marina where you can sit back and sip ouzo and watch the world go by. At night literally thousands of young people come out of god-only-knows-where, and they walk the square until the wee hours of the morning. On the beaches to the left and right of the town are restaurants right down on the sand, and since the Greeks eat late, usually 10:30 p.m. to midnight, these beaches are busier than a one-legged man in a sack race, all night long.

After leaving Nafpaktos we sailed toward the Corinth Canal and found a few more really great anchorages. On the island of Trizonia, there was a small taverna run by a couple of retired cruisers from Ireland, which specialized in Texas chili. Then there was a couple of great little hidden coves near Galaxidion for overnight stays. One of our favorite stops was at three little islands, hardly more than rocks, actually, called Alkyonidon Nisoi. Here we anchored between the rocks, and found one small home on one rock, and an old abandoned monastery on another. This is only about 15 miles from Corinth and the famous canal. In the morning we sailed into the city of Corinth.

It was here we met Tommy, and Tommy is one very interesting dude. We were side tied to the quay at the park right smack dab in downtown Corinth. In the afternoon folks would walk the park and stop to take pictures of the boat, or just to try and talk to us (it was all Greek to us!). Just before sunset this guy stands there looking at the boat, and before long he's aboard the LOST SOUL and we are old friends. His apartment overlooks the quay, and he's from Chicago. He is in politics, has made a lot of influential friends, done favors for people and has good connections.

Our new friend from Chicago took us under his wing, and for the next few days we met the owners of some of the best restaurants, and were stuffed to the gills with the finest, biggest, most delicious meals ever served in Greece. One night it was a meat house, then a fish place, and the owners all gave us personal service. Seems he's connected in Greece, too! After a couple of days he came with us to go for a ride through the Corinth Canal.

Some ladies from Redondo were to meet us in Corinth but did a no show, so we were left to our own devices for ten days until our next crew was flying in. It bummed us out, because so many people had wanted to come with us, and here we were with empty bunks through some of the best cruising in Greece. Also they had our mail with them, including poor Luke's college schedule, so he ended up flying home without knowing where he was to live, what classes he had or anything.

The Corinth Canal was a real trip, and about as expensive as Trump's divorce settlement. It cost 59,000 Drachmas which is around $280 just to motor the 3½ miles through the canal. And we thought the Panama Canal was expensive. But it was a real trip cruising waters where the Roman emperors had started digging with Jewish slaves back when Moses was doing the backstroke across the Red Sea! You could still see the craters from when it was bombed in World War II. At the end of the canal Danny, our crew for the previous six weeks, left with our new friend Tommy and went back to Corinth for a couple days before flying back to London and then home.

We headed out into the ancient Aegean Sea. I'm glad I didn't sleep through those history lessons. What a kick to sail the seas of the *Iliad* and the *Odyssey*! To say that we were more than a little excited would have been an understatement.

Forward Into History

> ◄━━━━━━

O ur first stop was in a little bay on the Peloponnese Peninsula called Dimani, where we ran into a retired U.S. Navy captain now living there. He gave us some tips on the Aegean, and in the morning we headed out for a small set of islands called the Angistri. We found a little taverna on a small bay all by itself and it looked almost like Polynesia with the white sand beaches and crystal blue waters, but with the added bonus of Greek food and mass quantities of German tourists wearing butt floss bathing suits for the crew's afternoon viewing pleasure.

In the morning we headed over to the small island of Aegina to see if the ladies who were supposed to have joined us in Corinth had made it in to our second rendezvous point. No such luck. When we have people fly in to join us, we always have a backup plan for a week later, just in case of travel problems. This time both rendezvous failed. We later learned they were having too much fun getting lucky in Mykonos, and had stayed there, leaving our mail in a hotel room. We never did get it.

We were stern tied to the wharf in Aegina, right in the middle of town, and were incredulous at what we found there. In the evening the streets were closed off to auto traffic, and only pedestrians and horse drawn carriages were allowed. All night long and into the wee hours of the morning folks would stroll the wharf, stopping at the sidewalk cafes. The ladies were dressed to kill in the latest fashions and the men were decked out in their best. People watching was at its zenith in Aegina. We met a displaced American backpacking through Europe and Africa. We kidnapped him to sail with us to another town called Vathi (there are actually a lot of towns in Greece named Vathi; it means "Deep Water."). This one consisted of a marina that would hold two boats, and two tavernas. Not exactly a metropolis, but very pretty and set at the base of a high tree-covered mountain.

We hopped to a few other places near the island of Hydra, and then headed back to Aegina, only this time to the east side. Here is where the Temple of Aphaea is located. This is the best preserved temple in Greece, dating from 300-400 B.C. That's not much older than some of the cheese we've been eating! In any case, to get there Jody and I rented a couple of motor scooters.

Now I want you to picture a 300+ pound tattooed biker astride a 45cc bright yellow moped. I just hope my friends at *Easyrider* didn't have any cameramen nearby. We had a great time riding around, and the next day we decided to make a quick trip to Athens.

Did I say quick? We pulled into Zea Marina in downtown Athens at about noon, gasping for air in the dense smog. By 3 p.m. we cast off our dock lines while stuffing groceries away, and headed out away from civilization, to where we could breathe. You can't believe the air in Athens. It's worse than Los Angeles in the 50s.

In the time we were there we located a new fuel pump and a backup, loaded up with a zillion dollars worth of groceries, downed enough Big Macs at the Greek McDonalds to choke Godzilla, and cast off before the port authorities got around to clearing us in or out.

We found a small uncharted island (well, we didn't have a chart of it!) about five miles off the coast and anchored in a well-protected little niche where the water was blue and so was the air. We were all alone as we spent a beautiful night looking back on the brilliant lights of Athens, and the brown-grey skies. In the morning we discovered why no one else was anchored in this neat little bay. It seems the ferry traffic in the morning passes just a mile off the coast, and the swells start coming in and knocking you around as if you were Mike Tyson's girlfriend. By 8 a.m. we were motoring towards our next anchorage, Sounion, where we were to meet our friends John and Lorri out of San Diego.

We've Reached our Goal

➤◄

S ounion was the place that we set sail for when we left the Pacific. It was the purpose for this trip—as if you need a reason to cruise anywhere!

As we sailed through Polynesia, we started to think about where in the world we really wanted to go after seeing the South Pacific. We decided that we should sail to pay our respects to the Temple of Poseidon, and that, it seems, was located at the Bay of Sounion, at the end of the Greek mainland. Now we're here!

On the top of the point, overlooking the sea, is the Temple of Poseidon, the Greek God of the Sea. It was built in 444 B.C. and most of it still stands today. Since I live on the sea, and have Poseidon tattooed on my chest, it seemed only right that we make our pilgrimage.

Jody and I climbed the mount at dawn and paid homage to the great sea god. We even bought a bronze icon and mounted it in the main saloon of the LOST SOUL, to protect us on our future journeys. After the others aboard had visited the temple we hoisted anchor once again, and headed north, to a large bay on the mainland where we could get supplies.

John and Lorri had arrived on time, and Luke was leaving us after being with us for over four months. Woody took a bus with him as far as Athens so they could visit the Acropolis, and then left Luke to catch his flight home to Canada. We missed him ten minutes after he left the boat. He had crewed with us in the South Pacific, and then again across the Atlantic and into the Med. He was family.

We anchored in our first Aegean Island, Kea, and found out once and for all why the Greek Islands are so popular as a cruising ground. The anchorage was completely surrounded by land and looked like an Alpine lake. At the water's edge was a small village with tavernas located right on the waterfront. After an evening downing the local brew and watching people, we spent the night on a velvet pond.

In the morning we caught a bus up the mountain to the village, which is in a crevasse about three miles up a winding road. Most of the older cities on the Greek Islands were built up on hills. It seems the pirates used to like to borrow things, like women, and it was easier to protect a hill than a port or beach.

We went in search of the lion of Kea. After winding our way through stairways and paths, we got totally lost. We stopped a young Greek lad to ask for directions, and found out he was a British punk rocker whose parents had sent him here to keep him out of trouble. He sullenly showed us the spot on the hill where we'd find the "lion," and wandered away muttering under his breath something about spending his summer bored out of his gourd pointing out the Whining Pussycat to a bunch of stupid American tourists.

We hiked passed the cemetery and about ¼ mile on, just after we passed the goatherd on his donkey leading a bunch of goats to graze, we found the Whining Pussycat. This 2600-year old sculpture is the oldest known Greek sculpture on the island, and it sits out in a hillside field. No gates, no fences. It just sits there.

We wandered back down the path, stopping at the water outlet to cool off in the crystal clear water coming out of the side of the mountain. All of a sudden the U.S. and civilization seemed a million miles away. Still in a semi-trance we wandered the twisting paths through the village and found a cool taverna where we had a Greek salad. We realized where we were, and loved it. The 12,000 miles to get here from our home port was now ancient history, and this was our reality.

Later that day we swam in the clear waters of the Aegean, and that evening, once again, we sat at the outdoor taverna, talking with the locals and enjoying the real Greece.

While anchored in Merikah, on the island of Kithnos, I discovered that Jody had finally gone over the edge. She was lying there reading and there were flies (they are everywhere in Greece) crawling on her and she wasn't swatting them off. I asked her why, and she calmly informed me that when they walked on her it was like being tickled, and she liked it. She's been at sea too long!

Dr. Scott Geller, who was soon to become known alternately as Disco Doc and Dr. Klutz, flew in to meet us in Kithnos. The next day we sailed over to the Island of Siros. We rented four mopeds and took turns exploring the island. Talk about a funny sight! One poor guy almost went off the road he was laughing so hard. I guess he never saw a large biker riding a moped, complete with cut-off Harley shirt and tattoos.

John and Lorri disappeared for the day, but we were used to not seeing them. We'd started calling them the honeymooners. Has something to do with the way they keep locked in their cabin. It isn't too bad for me and Jody, as we have our own head in our rear cabin, but poor Woody and Disco Doc have to wait for them to finish doin' the parallel cha-cha to use the forward head, and sometimes it takes 'em awhile! They not only keep the forward cabin busy, but when they go ashore they do it on the beaches, in old ruins, and once on the throne of an ancient temple on a hillside. Isn't love grand? 'Course the tourists love it too, as they walk around a secluded bend and see John's lily white buns pumping like some demented oil well.

While heading down the coast of Siros we came upon some interesting caves, so we dropped our hook to investigate. The caves were not on any of the guidebooks or cruising guides, and we could take the dinghy 300 feet into them. It was darker than a banker's heart in there, and even with a searchlight we could barely make our way in. This was perfect for the honeymooners, who made like rabbits once again until we finally had to send out Disco Doc in the kayak with a spotlight and a bucket of cold water to find them. He got a hell of a show, but he brought them back. It was probably the shock of the glowing white buns bouncing like a couple of albino turtles doing pushups on speed in the darkness of the cave that put him into the Dr. Klutz category, because from that moment on he started to drop his drinks, kick over other folks beers; he even managed to knock over a bowl of watermelon on the deck. That was just before he kicked over the deck table with the ashtray on it, and right after he knocked John's beer across the deck.

That night, in the port of Tinos, the great alcohol fog enveloped the LOST SOUL. It started a little after 11 p.m. The crew had gone off to find some adventure, while Jody and I stayed aboard and listened to a little blues from Doug McCloud. Just after midnight we heard a bang-thud and went up to find John face down on the deck. His honeymoon partner, Lorri, had flown back to San Diego that day. Woody and Dr. Klutz found him stumbling around in a bar and brought him home.

At 3 a.m. I awoke to what sounded like a herd of elephants on the deck. After the bar closed, Woody and Disco Doc had herded seven mini-skirted Belgian foxes aboard. I don't know who was more plastered, the girls or Woody and Dr. Disco. I did my best imitation of a Mad Dad, complete with bellowing expletives and soon the decks were cleared of excessive female pulchritude, leaving just the two finest with the shortest skirts and highest heels. At 5 a.m. I awoke again to the tippy-toeing of little feet as they left the boat to go to their hotel.

In order to live up to my image of a truly nasty guy, at 8 a.m. sharp I started the motor and woke everybody up (except John, who couldn't be awakened with an A-bomb in his ear) and we took off to explore the ancient world of Greece.

Delos was the center of the world back in the second millennium, about 1500 to 1200 B.C. The island offers a well-preserved look into the life of that time. The homes, with indoor plumbing, marble inlaid baths and unbelievable marble sculptures, are every bit as nice as those in Bel Air. The theater is a match for the Greek theater in Hollywood, and the huge marble lions that guarded the city are just plain awesome. We wandered among the ruins for hours and saw what it was like to live 3500 years ago.

After we left Delos we anchored in the south bay of Rinia, just two miles to the west of Delos. It is also known as Big Delos, and was part of the ancient center of the world. Velvet smooth water, white sand beaches, skies bigger than OJ's ego and a full moon with so much light you could see the shadow of the boat on the bottom. Phenomenal.

We headed over to Mykonos to meet some friends flying in and to drop John, the other honeymooner, off so he could fly home to Lorri. After all, it had been three days since they saw each other!

Mykonos is the most touristy of all the Greek islands. What's it really like? I guess some folks like it. It seems Mykonos has more fairies playing Butt Bongos than even Ibiza had. Of course that did make it easier for our crew to score.

The Meltemi

*H*ell night started out innocently enough, as hell nights do. Woody, John and Dr. Disco left Jody and me on the boat, anchored off the rocky shores of Mykonos, and took the dinghy in for a night of revelries and partying. Jody and I opted to stay on the boat and enjoy a good video and possibly some adult games. At a little before 5 a.m. I heard the depth alarm go off. Jody and I ran up on deck to find a 35-knot wind blowing out of the north. It was a meltemi, which we've heard a lot about, but until now hadn't had the privilege of experiencing. We were blowing into the rocks, dragging our anchor. We went to start the engine but the batteries were low, so we had to start the generator and wait five minutes for the charger to bring up the batteries. As we did that the boat drifted back until we were only feet from the rocks. As the motor started I noticed something missing. The dinghy! Our crew was still ashore.

As the sun came up Jody and I were re-anchoring for the fifth time. This time we let out 300 feet of chain in 50 feet of water, only to drift back again. There was no place to duck in out of the weather, and the seas were up to six feet and choppy. No way we could get an anchor to hold, and if we did it would be hell. We couldn't go the three miles to the lee of the island, because our crew was still out, and not only wouldn't they be able to find us, but if they did they couldn't take the dinghy across those seas. So for the next four hours, until well after 10 a.m., Jody and I motored back and forth in a full gale near the town quay, waiting for our wayward crew, who were having a wonderful time being soused out of their gourds.

A little after 10:30 a captain from another boat signaled

to us that there was a place we could pull in out of the seas, but it was right next to where the big ferries came in, and their prop wash might be a little troublesome.

As we tied to the quay my wayward crew finally showed up, about as useless as teats on a boar hog. But we did manage to get tied to the quay. Not half an hour later Dale, Mickey and Rhonda showed up. They were the folks that would be joining us for the next two weeks. Woody, John and Dr. Disco promptly glommed onto Rhonda (she's single) and spirited her off to show her the sights. The rest of the day I sat anchor watch as my crew got even more blotto.

Of course there are advantages in having a degenerate crew. About 4 p.m. they came stumbling back aboard and passed out in various places and positions, Woody in the storm room, Scott below, and John in the hammock on the bow. Now I may have forgotten to mention this, but we were tied up at the ferry terminal waiting for the meltemi to die, so literally thousands of people were parading by the boat every hour, as they left the ferries and we probably had plenty of video shots of our boat.

The most videoed event was the half hour it took for John to fall out of the hammock. First his arm, then his head, and soon his face was on the deck, looking like he was French kissing it, and his ass was in the air; then, as time went on, he rolled the rest of the way onto the deck. His sunglasses were cocked on his head, and you could see his drool looking like snail tracks where his face had slid along the deck.

There are days when you dream of singlehanding once again. That night most of the crew stayed aboard nursing various sized melons on their shoulders, except Disco Doc. He was out all night, and at 5 a.m. brought two bimbos aboard to party some more! Even Woody and John were impressed with his staying power. Later that morning we bid adieu to John, who was flying home with a hangover. Then we cast off and those of us who were able waved goodbye and good riddance to Mykonos.

The next day we spent anchored in the south bay of Rinia, on a small and beautiful uninhabited beach with white sand and crystal clear blue water. Once again we remembered what cruising is all about. We dropped our new crew off at Delos in the morning so they could enjoy the ancient site, and in the afternoon we sailed the downwind run to Paros. With the meltemi blowing behind us at 25 knots we headed downwind fast.

Paros was an excellent anchorage to get out of the meltemi. They say the meltemi can blow out of the north up to 45 knots and blow for either one or two weeks. After two and a half days it started to subside. While we waited it out we rented some more mopeds, or slo-peds as we like to refer to them, and made a circumnavigation of the island. It's starting to be a regular thing to rent a bunch of slo-peds, and I am even getting used to the laughs and derisive remarks I hear. What the hell, I'm having fun.

Each night at midnight Disco Doc would head ashore to sample the various disco palaces, which seem to be on every island. We managed to find a couple of good topless beaches, so boredom didn't set in, and Dale, Mickey and Rhonda found a valley full of butterflies.

Well, they say they did. I still think they found a valley full of odd smoking herbs, and just think they found butterflies.

The last night before leaving Paros we had dinner at a small taverna on the beach, and were treated to some local Metaxa Brandy before we departed. Nasty stuff.

Once again Disco Doc hit the shore at midnight, and we all hit the hay. As the meltemi died in the morning we headed south to a small anchorage between Paros and Adiparos. This is where all the pirates used to hang out in the fourteenth, fifteenth and sixteenth centuries. No wonder we felt at home.

The next day we dropped Disco Doc off in Adiparos and sailed in the meltemi south to the island of Ios. This is the land of the naked babe, and it didn't take long to find 'em. Actually the first folks we saw were naked dudes, so the ladies were busy with the binoculars. We anchored off the first night, and then went stern to the quay the second day. We rented some more slo-peds and the LOST SOUL gang was riding again. We raided the southern beaches and came back with plenty of booty. Okay, we came back with sunburned tongues and almost as much exposed film as there was exposed flesh on the beaches.

We heard that there was no good anchorage in Thira, which is the island they say was Atlantis, and the town of Santorini is a must see, so one day Dale, Mickey, Jody and I took a ferry for the twenty miles across the channel. A 300-foot boat that I didn't have to worry about. It was great.

In Thira we had to take a bus up the 400-foot high sheer cliffs to get to the city. The last thing on earth you ever want to do there is get in an overcrowded bus on a hot day. Let me put it this way: Their deodorant doesn't cut it. We were jammed like a bunch of sardines into this bus where the temperature was about 110 degrees. We were surrounded with a group of people I am sure belong to some cult that believes if you take a bath your sex organs fall off. Poor Jody was jamming her nose into my armpits to get a breath of fresh air. It was that bad!

Santorini was unbelievable. A city perched on top of sheer cliffs that dropped hundreds of feet to the crystal blue Mediterranean. The streets were narrow flagstone paths; you could touch both sides with your hands at the same time, and they wound haphazardly among the buildings and cliffs.

We got to take a ferry ride back to Ios where we'd left the boat. We sailed in a meltemi (35 knots of wind out of the north) to the south shore of Thira. There was a good anchorage there after all. Once again we visited Santorini and were re-convinced that it is the most picturesque city any of us had ever seen. That evening we had dinner on the beach at a small taverna, and at dawn set sail for the island of Crete.

Iraklion, Crete. How does one describe it? Dirty, disgust-ing, ugly. Yes, all of those things, and more. The harbor is the worst I have ever been in. It makes Ensenada look civilized. No marina, no anchorage and no services. What it lacks in charm and grace it makes up for in dirt and inconvenience.

While in this large cesspool we started to have some trou-bles with our generator again, so we walked the mile and a half to get off the wharf they wanted us to tie to, and found a mechanic. To get to a phone was a couple of miles, and to have a beer the same. That sobered Woody up.

There was one socially redeeming factor however: the an-cient city of Knossos, believed to have been destroyed by the exploding of Atlantis. It has been preserved for centuries, and the murals and mosaics are absolutely perfect.

We said goodbye to Dale, Mickey and Rhonda and were joined by Shawn, who was signing on as crew for the Atlantic crossing and beyond.

Actually it wasn't too bad having our stay in Iraklion the last in Greece, because we had enjoyed the rest of Greece so much we might not have left. As it was we had to say no to the $3.50 per gallon fuel and hope we'd make it to Malta on the 150 gallons still in our tanks, and that it would be cheaper there. We did have to pop for some $15 a gallon oil for the en-gine and generator, though.

We also had to have the engine heads welded and a new valve custom made for our generator. Try getting that done in Greek sometime! We ended our stay in a most enjoyable way. In Iraklion we came upon some great people. Greg, a mechanic we ran into, pulled a miracle when he took our cracked generator head and burned valve and in one day had it welded, machined and a new valve custom made. All for under $375, including his labor.

The night before we left we met Captain Bernard on the 100-foot motoryacht GALADRIEL, and while we were exchanging information we learned he was with Jacques Cousteau on CALYPSO as first mate, and eventually as captain. He gave us a tour of his boat, and some neat tricks to ease our entry if we sailed into Malta, where we planned on heading the next morning. As it turns out, and as usual with the LOST SOUL, our plans went right out the porthole the next morning. We untied from the dock and headed west. After a pretty good sail of 60 miles we entered the ancient port of Hania so our new crewman Shawn could get a glimpse of Greece before we left it. As we turned into the harbor we were hit right on the nose with 35 knots of wind. We got tied to the quay just as a three-day storm hit. Being just slightly brighter than your average slug we opted to stay in port and drink beer as opposed to getting the poop knocked out of us trying to fight a gale head on.

When the winds died down we paid the $80 harbor fee and sailed some 20 miles to an old pirate hideout on the west end of Crete. There we found a wreck, a white sand beach, and a fortress built high atop an island that looked like something out of *Captains Courageous*. It was great anchorage, and not a soul around.

The next day we started our trek across the Mediterranean. We knew the weather could be as fickle as Heidi Fleiss at a millionaires' party, so we planned a course where we could duck in at the first sign of a storm. It was lucky we did. We took off at dawn and by late afternoon we had made about 75 miles.

The Gates of Hell

C ape Taineron is where the mythical Gates of Hades are and, as we approached it, we started to believe the myth. The wind started at 20 knots, then went to 25 and finally 35 knots, with seas bigger than Madonna's opinion of herself.

We looked for a place to tuck in and found one, and in the cruising guide, right there in black and white, it showed a large cave. It is, and has always been, known as the Gates of Hades.

This cape is where the Ionian and the Aegean meet, and it is world famous as a place to be reckoned with, or even avoided by smart people. That left us out! In fact, in the *Odyssey* this is where Odysseus was blown south to the land of the lotus eaters. We were hit with high winds and seas but never saw a lotus or its eater. We were truly bummed.

We pulled into a small anchorage and looked for a place to anchor. The bottom sloped pretty steeply to the shore, but we gave it a try. On our second attempt we had dropped the hook in 20 feet of water, backing down on it, and let out about 250 feet of chain. By the time it was out we were sitting in 100 feet of water. That was 12 to one scope from where we anchored, but only 2.5 to one where we sat. I figured the average would handle it, so we ate dinner and turned in.

At two in the morning I was awakened by Woody. He'd gotten up to drain his lizard, and found we were drifting in 350 feet of water. As we'd slept our anchor had drifted off the shelf.

Marvelous, simply marvelous! Just what you like to wake up to. We started the engine, hoisted the anchor, and headed out to sea. It seemed to make the most sense, since we were up anyway.

There we are a day later, halfway across the Ionian, 120

miles from land in either direction. The sun is coming up and it is calm. I'm talking water flatter than Twiggy. Anyhow, it's 6 a.m. and I'm on watch while we're motoring, doing about seven knots.

All of a sudden I smell smoke. Smoke is not a good thing on a boat in mid-sea. I scrambled down the steps and opened the engine room door, and was instantly enveloped in thick smoke.

I shut down the engine and the rest of the crew came scrambling to see what's up. It wasn't a fire, but we had blown a one-foot-long, 3-inch-diameter exhaust hose for which we paid $80 in Cannes just two months earlier. This is one of the few things I don't carry a backup for. For the next two hours we sat becalmed as we jury-rigged a replacement by cutting down our anti-siphon loop and using the hose from it. There is nothing quite as much fun as trying to get a 3-foot exhaust hose off a cast iron fitting it's been on for 11 years. It's like gettin' panty hose off on a first date.

Two hours later it was fixed, and we were on our way once again. We cleared the Straits of Messina at dawn, passing the tip of the boot of Italy where it kicks Sicily. We were making good time with no adverse winds so we opted to keep going without a stop. We passed the island of Volcano that afternoon, which is one of five islands we would pass that day. All are active volcanos. Great for the nerves.

Two days later we pulled into Cagliari on the southern tip of Sardinia for a day's rest. We had made it halfway across the Med non-stop, but our newly fixed generator had another problem.

When supermechanic Greg had fixed the burned valve and cracked head, he didn't have a new head gasket to put on. After two hours of running the head gasket blew, blowing three liters of dirty oil all over the generator room. We found a mechanic in Cagliari and tried to tell him what was wrong, but he didn't speak English and we didn't speak Italian. An hour later he said he couldn't fix it.

We spent the night at the harbor getting some needed rest, or at least Jody and I did. Woody and Shawn went out with a guy they met on a boat from Canada, and stumbled in at dawn, just as I was getting ready to shove off. We got off the dock just as they fell into a deep sleep.

A couple of days later we pulled into Ibiza, Spain to get our generator head gasket fixed again and spent two nights recovering from the 1,100 mile jaunt across the Med. At dawn we headed out for Gibraltar. We sailed downwind all the way to Cabo de Gata, where we made our final turn for the last 150 miles to Gibraltar.

We turned the corner to the west, with a good breeze blowing us toward Gibraltar. The sun was a fireball on the horizon, and I was with heavy heart to be leaving the Med. All the hassles, the engine and generator problems, the high costs and the storms, none of that meant a thing. We had sailed the same seas that Columbus left from. We had followed the path of Ulysses and Odysseus. We had trodden the streets of Pompeii, of Delos and Crete where men like us lived 3500 years ago. And we were a part of that history.

While we were tied up in Gibraltar a high settled in over Spain and the winds whipped up to Force 9 in the channel, up to 65 knots. We opted to sit it out at the marina. While there we re-made some acquaintances with people like Tom on a 70-foot Oceana and Craig and Mark, whom we'd last seen in Puerto Vallarta on the 42-foot yacht PANDAROSA. Tom we last met in the Azores, and before that in Mexico. Craig and Mark sailed out of the Kona Kai International Yacht Club in San Diego, and when last seen bought a used autopilot brain from me in Puerto Vallarta, three years earlier.

There I was, sitting on the dock in Gibraltar rebuilding a

head that had decided to stop swallowing stuff, and this guy walks up and starts talking motorcycles. Kewl! I spent many years riding them, and soon we were aboard LOST SOUL downing quantities of cold and sudsy brew.

I figured he was a crewman off one of the yachts. He was from Malaysia, and we just kind of hit it off from the start of our conversation. You know how sometimes people just klick. Anyway, after about an hour I am bidding this guy adieu, and he invites me for a cold one on his boat. I of course, being a true ugly American, assume he is crew, and fluff it off.

A while later Jody and I are walking to the phone on the docks, and we see this unbelievable 72-foot Swan named JUGRA. My mouth is drooling prolifically as we pass it, taking in all the little whistles and bells on this multi-million dollar sled.

All of a sudden my little friend Idris sticks his head out of a hatch and invites us aboard. Figuring the owners aren't aboard, I jump at a chance to see this beautiful boat.

As we walk the deck checking out the automatic winches and other neat stuff, Idris goes below. A few seconds later he comes back up wearing a Harley shirt, and we sit in the cockpit talking boats and bikes. I am getting nervous, waiting for the owners to tell us to get off the boat.

Then Mark and Clair from New Zealand stick their heads up and start bringing munchies and cold brew up. Must be a neat owner to allow their Malaysian deck hand to have friends aboard, huh?

I, being unbelievably adroit at sticking my size-13 foot into my overactive mouth, mention this. It is then that Idris informs me that, no, he is not crew. Actually, it is his boat, and he is sailing to Daytona Beach for Bike Week, on his way to sailing around the world.

His full name is Prince Idris Shah, Raja Muda of Selangor. He sponsors the Raja Muda Regatta out of the Royal Se-

langor Yacht Club in Malaysia, and we are invited to participate. He even offered me one of his Harleys to ride while there.
We found that this was the royal yacht, and he was a genuine
prince type dude. It was a little weird, but I soon got used to it,
and after awhile he was just another biker-boater. There aren't
many of us out there, so we hang close. To this day I still jok-
ingly call him our Malaysian Deck Hand.

As he was on his way to Daytona I called my friend Keith
at *Easyriders* Magazine and got him a room there. It seems
that even a Prince can't get a room in Daytona on Bike week,
and he was incredulous when he found I could.

We managed to fix all the little things that had happened
since the last port (generator, main engine exhaust, mainsail,
coat of varnish, head, etc.) and stocked up for the ensuing
couple of months. We didn't know what we'd find in the Canary Islands, and after the hurricanes in the Caribbean we
didn't know what supplies would be like when we got there,
either. Better safe than sorry, so we got plenty of food, booze
and toilet paper.

The winds finally calmed down, and on Saturday at dawn
we took off. JUGRA was right behind us as were MIRAGE from
England and RHAPSODY from Australia. Also we had PAN-
DAROSA from San Diego and another boat out of Florida. We
had a regular flotilla.

Of course the real flotilla was coming about three days
behind us. A rally called the ARC consisted of over 200 boats
crossing the Atlantic together. They were leaving the Canary
Islands on November 19. Not wanting to be bumped into by
numerous jittery sailboats, we planned an earlier departure.

Our stalwart crew going through the Canal

Belize. Yeah, we can do that!

Leaving Xcalak, Mexico. Almost more adventure than we can stand

Anchored off the Baths in Virgin Gorda,
British Virgin Islands

The view from Virgin Gorda's

Legal graffiti on the Horta Docks in the Azores

In the background is our supply ship, the VIRGINIAN,
as we pose with Captain Ingo

We cannot recommend decadence as a
way of life, but it works for us. Aboard the
VIRGINIAN in the Azores

We figure Luke has been at sea too long, as we land in Gibraltar

The 700-year-old port of Villefranche-sur-Mer

Anchored off the beach at Cannes

Two friends reunited after 35 years

The walled city of Calvi, Corsica

Bonifacio. The safest anchorage in Corsica

Anchored off the island of Oxia, Greece

Going through the Corinth Canal

Anchored in Mykonos

The mystical island of Santorini

New crew in Antigua

Just another day in paradise

The volcano at Montserrat as seen from Antigua

New Year's Eve. Is this any way to treat a crown prince?

Filming a documentary off the coast of Dominica

The beautiful Tobago Cays in the Grenadines

We arrive in the San Blas Islands

Being greeted by the Kuna Indians in San Blas

Goodbye Med—Hello Atlantic

At sunset the first night out we were passed by Prince Idris on JUGRA under full sail. Nothing quite looks like a 72-foot Swan under full sail. We sailed passed Tangiers and Casablanca, and motored in a dead calm as we passed from Morocco to the Western Sahara Desert. The Moroccan Navy came up to us and had us slow down, but they decided we were okay, and let us go on our way.

On our arrival in the Canary Islands we went to the easternmost island of Lanzarote, and as we entered the marina we found it was full. JUGRA had come in the day before, and had a tie-up, so we side tied to them for our one-day stay.

That evening we had a little birthday party for Prince Idris' sailing guru, Captain M.J.F. Vroon from Holland, who was so embarrassed by the whole thing he glowed a wondrous shade of red most of the night. The next day he wore his birthday present from the LOST SOUL, a skull and crossbones T-shirt. He loved it.

We split up the next day. JUGRA sailed to the next marina while we went in search of some exhaust hose to fix our Mickey Mouse fixit job. A few days later we joined them again.

When we arrived the marina was filled with boats waiting for Jimmy Cornell's ARC, and this year there were well over 200 boats waiting to go. What they do is cross all together. I guess there's safety in numbers but it seems to me they would be colliding with each other there were so many boats. Once again we couldn't find a place to tie up, and then we saw JUGRA with a sign on its outer lifeline. It said "Reserved for the LOST SOUL." We side tied once again and had a great time with the prince and his crew. I became the Royal Bodyguard, Jody the Royal Bartender, and we had a royal great time. One night Idris took us to dinner at a great little place inland, and when we were already in the car ready to leave, the proprietor came running out with a tray of drinks for us.

Our stay in the Canary Islands was starting to take its toll. After weeks of trying to keep up with our cruising partners on JUGRA, we were getting to be in pretty sad shape.Our crew, Woody and Shawn, would go out every night with the prince and his crew. They'd come stumbling in near daylight, and were heard to snivel more than once when asked to do some chores aboard the LOST SOUL.

Jimmy Cornell's ARC was waiting to take off across the Atlantic, and we sure didn't want to be in the middle of all those boats. With Prince Idris in agreement, we set our plans to leave a couple of weeks prior to the ARC.

About an hour out I had one of the biggest scares of my entire sailing life. We were hard on a starboard tack, heeled over pretty good because of the tight headwinds. We were motorsailing into it, and I was on watch. I was sitting contemplating my navel, when all of a sudden an anchored fishing boat slid past us not more than five feet away.

It had been hidden by the sail, and I just plain didn't see it. As it popped into view I started to figure real fast how I could say it wasn't my fault, as the fishermen were hurling invective in our direction in some language that was Greek to me. Of course there is no way to blame an anchored vessel if you are in a collision with it while under sail, so I just turned a little redder than an overripe tomato, and swallowed my pride, as I was blasted by all aboard for not watching.

As we headed southwest we got hit right in the face with a southwest wind. That, of course, was precisely the direction we wanted to go. The first day we spent fighting our way against 20- to 25-knot winds right on the nose. What else would you expect from a crossing that is always described as a milk run?

A few hours behind us JUGRA left harbor, and a little later we were commiserating over the unbelievable headwinds. Then we got the news. A late hurricane was blowing just a few degrees above us. All of a sudden 25-knot headwinds didn't seem so bad.

We watched our weatherfaxes come in and each one showed the hurricane heading off slightly more to the north. It was going to miss us. The next night it was with great pleasure that we motored through the calm, where normally we would be having a downwind sail. Better than fight a hurricane.

JUGRA pulled ahead and I was hardly jealous at all. We kept in touch by single sideband radio, and compared our wind and seas as we headed southwest across the Atlantic. We got some tail winds for a change and for the first time ever on the LOST SOUL we did a wing-and-wing with spinnakers. We had our 2,500-square-foot spinnaker off the racing sled Blondie hanked on the starboard side sheeted to the end of the main boom, and another spinnaker sheeted to the end of the mizzen boom routed to the top of the mizzen mast like a mizzen staysail, on the port side. The wind was right behind us and we were cranking out eight knots in zero knot of apparent wind.

Now there are those of you who would say this is very economical, saving money on fuel like this, but since we put three holes in the big chute, broke two snapblocks (at $150 each!) and lost another piece of teak off our bow pulpit during our jibe, in the end it was not economical at all, but heaps of fun. I figure the savings a negative $500 for the afternoon, but it's unreal feeling 42 tons of boat sleighing downwind at 8 to

10 knots with no real wind. We really felt great that evening when we found out JUGRA motored because they didn't think there was enough wind to sail. Hah!

For the next few days we sailed in light winds or motor-sailed into the center of the Atlantic. JUGRA was slightly above us at 23 degrees while we tried to stay to the southern track at 20 degrees. Slowly they outdistanced us. A week into the crossing and they were about 225 miles in front of us. They blew a spinnaker, we tore ours, so we were pretty well matched as we waited for the tradewinds to hit us.

My personal hell day started on November 8 at precisely 9:20 a.m. We were about 1600 miles from Antigua and 1100 miles from the Canary Islands. The night before was pretty normal. We sailed under our light air sail with main and mizzen up as well, but at 2 a.m. the wind decided to take the night off so we snuffed the big light air sail and turned on the motor. I had trouble getting back to sleep, but I did at about 5 a.m., and at 6 was awakened for my watch. At 9 a.m. I was relieved and went down below for a little catch-up sleep.

About five minutes after I dozed off Jody woke me to tell me our batteries were down below 12 volts. That news is about as welcome as a dinner invitation from Jeffrey Dahmer. I found the alternator belt was shredding, so, with no wind, we drifted as we shut off the engine for repairs. Of course to change an alternator belt on the LOST SOUL you must first remove the two belts to the refrigeration compressor. Mickey Mouse engineering at its best.

After waking both Woody and Shawn (why should they sleep when I don't!), we got it done, with only a minimal amount of swearing and busted knuckles. Then we hit the starter button. Oops! Not enough juice to start the engine. But we did manage to clear the memories on our SatNav and two

GPS, as well as all our digital clocks due to the massive drop in volts when we hit the starter.

So we first had to start the generator to charge the batteries. No problem, right?

Wrong! When we were running the generator the night before it shut down by itself, so I decided I'd check it out in the morning. Needless to say, the generator wouldn't start, but while we cranked it we managed to back up the water of the cooling system into the cylinder heads.

So now we got to take off the generator room door, pull the water lines from the generator, crank her over for awhile, then run the preheat to dry the cylinders, and finally start her up. She ran pretty well, so we charged the batteries on the main system and soon started the main engine.

But as we did it we heard Shawn yelling like a banshee up on deck. We went topside to find him fighting a large dorado on the fishing tackle, and hollering for help with the handline, where another big dorado was fighting.

Good news? Not on the LOST SOUL. As I pulled in the handline I landed the 15-pound dorado, only to watch him spit out the hook, spit some blood on my deck, and then give me the big eye, as he danced off the deck leaving me empty handed. But wait, we still had dinner on the other line. I went around to the port side and Woody handed me the rod around the rigging to get us closer to midships.

Yeah, you got it. The damned fish looked at me and seemed to say, "Hey, you let my buddy go, so I'm outta here!" and he dropped off the hook and swam away. You could have frozen ice with the looks in my crew's eyes. I grabbed a pillow off the aft deck and headed to the foredeck where I could be alone with my misery.

As I passed the winch it grabbed my shorts, ripping my last good pair, and as I turned to release them from where they were stuck, the pillow, which had been with us for over 40,000 miles around the world, fell overboard.

Those of you who have wondered what it's like out in the middle of the big blue would probably like to know what's out there. Well, just like at home, you get the good days and the bad ones.

At the halfway point, 1,350 miles from land in any direction, we were starting to get a little worried. We had still not gotten the tradewinds, and were motoring through calm waters. Our fuel was starting to run low, and we sailed whenever we could maintain three knots of speed. That's a little slower than most people walk.

Can you imagine walking across the Atlantic?

Our fuel ran out with 688 miles still to go to landfall. We were sitting down to dinner when the engine coughed, and then died. There wasn't a breath of wind.

We spent the rest of the evening just drifting in the dead calm of the night. Come the morning and we got a little wind and started the long slow haul to Antigua.

We had saved 20 gallons of fuel for our generator so we wouldn't run out of electricity, but other than that we were on wind power.

The last 130 miles was the hardest. We would be becalmed, then hit with 25 knots of wind in a squall, then have giant screaming grey squalls dump copious amounts of rainwater on us, and of course the wind would shift 50 to 60 degrees, making us tack and jibe over and over again. It felt like we were pushing the LOST SOUL into harbor. The day before we saw land we landed two blue marlin, and had lots of fish jerky and a great ciopino.

At 10:02 a.m. on November 19, just 19½ days after leaving the Canary Islands, Woody shouted "land-ho!" Our crossing was a little over 2,750 miles, and was done in what is considered "average" time. Of course they take an average of normal crossings, when the tradewinds are blowing. The hurricane that hit the Azores just as we left the Canary Islands turned the weather upside down for our crossing, so the normal Atlantic high was an Atlantic low. We never did see the tradewinds, and ended up motoring over 1,100 miles before we ran out of fuel.

As we approached English Harbour we tried to start the engines so we could maneuver, but had no luck. The starter just moaned a little, and ground to a halt. Of course we were about to enter the harbor, so we had to start the generator for awhile in order to charge the batteries enough to start the main. Hard to have that much fun.

It felt as if we had come home as we pulled into English Harbour in Antigua. Our plan was to hang out and fix all the stuff we couldn't get fixed in Europe, and generally take a vacation from our vacation.

Back in the Western Hemisphere

——————▶◀——————

*J*ody and I were walking down a white sand road which bordered the bright blue bay of Falmouth Harbour in Antigua. In front of us a reincarnation of Bob Marley, holding a banana tree on his lap and a joint the size of a $50 Cuban cigar in his hand, rode on the back of a jackass. He was pure Rastafarian, and there was no doubt at all that we were back in the West Indies.

It was almost like a homecoming after our 5,000-mile marathon from Crete through the Med and across the Atlantic. We settled into the Caribbean lifestyle with ease. We were tied up to Nelson's Dockyard; the famous Admiral Nelson built it, and his boat used to be tied up right where we were tied. Our first night ashore after the crossing we met some folks at Rock the Dock, which is the best bar on the harbor, and all of a sudden we were home.

Big Jim, whom I called Little Brother for awhile, and who later became Little Bother, is a big ol' Scotsman who has lived in Antigua for eight years and also keeps a house in Florida and in Scotland. He owns GT Pizza with his better half Judy, and Molly is their bartender. Molly has more piercings than a porcupine's mattress and her hair is spiked a la old Rod Stewart style, only hers is black. She and Jody hit it off right away. Molly lives with Guy. Guy, who is almost my age, owns the Rock the Dock and is a misplaced punk rocker from North Dakota, a sort of a cross between David Bowie and the boy next door. In all they made us feel at home from the moment we landed, and after a week there it was hard to leave. We had our generator and main engine worked on and had our mainsail re-stitched after the 17,000 miles we put on her since we left. We also had to fix the spinnaker as we tore her pretty good on the crossing. After ten days the generator was put back together, and it still did not work.

For four months we had worked on trying to fix the %$#@#$% thing and had spent over $2,500 in the trying. Now it adds up to $4,500 to fix a $5,000 generator *and the damn thing still didn't work!*

Since we need a generator to do little things like run the watermaker and the battery charger, we disconnected it and hauled it out of the boat. For the next two weeks we would sail around without it.

Since Woody had abandoned ship as soon as we arrived in Antigua to fly home and see his sweetie we had to fill the void. In order to get the most of our island cruise we kidnapped two sisters from Australia as additional crew. Jody, 20 and Kylie, 21 wanted to see the islands and we could use the extra bodies, ah, I mean hands. Once their gear was stashed down below we headed out to sail up-island to Five Islands Bay. Of course Gilligan (our new name for Shawn) was in such a state having two half naked bodies around, the first thing he did was wrap the halyard and then almost crank off one of the mast steps. For the next few days all he could do was piss himself, but soon things settled down to normal. Normal for the LOST SOUL anyway.

After three or four days we pulled into St. Johns, Antigua to check out for the next island. Big Jim drove over to say goodbye, and we had a small fete at the Crazy Horse. After we were sufficiently sotted, we crawled back to the boat and got some sleep for our big crossing, Antigua to St. Barts.

A full breeze of 18 knots filled our sails as we broad reached across the 75 miles to St. Barts. In our heads we pictured having cocktails with Mick and Cher at a small hideaway on this, the most private of the West Indies. As we tacked around the southern point these dreams turned to sour borscht. We were greeted with no less than three cruise ships anchored off, and about 100 sailboats. This place was about as private as the Happy Hooker's bedroom.

We anchored off between megayachts and dinghied ashore. Actually it was pretty nice. The food was great. One night we downed mass quantities of pizza, and the next day I had the pleasure of the best hamburger I'd seen since Fatburger.

The liquor stores in St. Barts are of the warehouse variety, and they are setup pretty neat. You walk into a small welcoming room, and there are bottles of just about every kind of booze you can think of, on shelves, with prices on 'em. Like a quart of rum for $19, or a fifth of vodka for $24. Only thing is, that's the price for *a case*!

We bought a couple cases of rum, one of vodka, some scotch, bourbon and gin, and a few cases of beer.

Now you want to talk about some catcalls? I want you to picture old lard-butt here, in a dinghy piled high with cases of booze, being held up by three gorgeous women in little bitty bikinis. As we passed the cruise ships on our way to the LOST SOUL I swear I heard the whole ship sigh with envy.

After three days of great snorkeling, swimming and sightseeing we headed a few miles up island to Colombier, which is a deserted white sand beach that people either have to sail into or hike. As we dropped anchor we had to pry the binoculars out of Gilligan's hands. Clothing was optional on the beaches, and it seemed that no one opted to wear any. After a half hour of listening to Gilligan try to convince our two Australian deckhands that no clothes were allowed on the beach (they didn't buy it!), we all went swimming and enjoyed a great day in a beautiful bay.

The sail to St. Kitts was great. A downwind run at 9 to 10

knots with all sails full. It was blowing 20 knots from behind us and I was actually starting to think that there really is such a thing as sailing downwind! We pulled into the lee of St. Kitts and were in absolute awe as we passed what has to be the sister island to Maui in Hawaii. Green sugar cane fields reaching up the side of a volcano and white sand beaches with waving palms. We hired a car once we got in and Jody and I did the tourist bit around the island. It was discovered by Columbus in 1493 and settled in the 1500s. Some of the original building sites are still being used, and there is a large fort on Brimstone hill which has been pretty well restored.

That night there was a Rasta party as Bunny Wailer (Bob Marley's old group) was giving a concert, and over a dozen Rasta bands showed up to participate. Shawn and the girls went, while Jody and I opted for a quieter evening aboard ship. There was so much ganja at the concert we almost got a contact high anchored out in the bay!

The next day we sailed a few miles down island to a hidden cove where we anchored and did some snorkeling, and in the morning we sailed to the neighboring island of Nevis.

Nevis is a volcanic island that looks like a sombrero, but it's all green. It is surrounded with white sand beaches and tall palm trees. Things were a little spendy there however. A box of cereal was Eastern Caribbean $18 (about U.S. $7) and Pringles were over U.S. $4 a package. We picked up a few supplies and then sailed down island to a deserted anchorage where the water was crystal clear and the sand looked like white sugar. It was like a living postcard.

From this paradise we sailed on a close reach, which is about as much fun as a mouse mating with an elephant, and sailed through six squalls with winds well up over gale force, and after copious amounts of rain drenched us we arrived in Montserrat.

Holidays in the Caribbean

━━━━━━▶◀━━━━━━

*M*ontserrat is a volcanic island that is having what you might call growing pains. There is a volcano going off as you read this. When we arrived the eastern portion of the island had been evacuated and we were told to move to the northwest to Old Road Bay to be out of danger. Leave it to the crew of the LOST SOUL to arrive just when an island is about to make like Krakatoa. For the next three days we were in true paradise. We fell in love with Montserrat. The people there are so friendly you'd think you just won the lottery. As we wandered the island people would stop to point out things of interest, or just to say hello. The first night the policeman who checked us in came by after work for dinner, and stayed for a video and late that night we felt as if we were saying goodbye to a friend as he left the boat. In the next few days everyone we met made us feel more at home than we had felt for years.

On the fourth day of our one-day stop we finally hoisted anchor. We kept looking back at Montserrat, saying to ourselves "We'll be back."

As it turned out that wasn't to be the case. Soon after we left the whole island was evacuated, and the volcano won the battle for possession of the island.

Leaving proved to be a little harder than we expected. As we cleared the south end of the island we were hit in the face with a *big* squall. Like 40-knot winds and drenching rain, and it was right between us and Antigua. Being true cruising sailors, we changed course and sailed south to Guadeloupe instead.

We anchored in Deshaies (I pronounced it Day-shits, they pronounced it Day-hey) on Guadeloupe and were once again

•━•

in frog country. If we didn't know it from the signs we'd have known it by the rude people. After a squall-filled crossing we sat at anchor for two days and had a movie marathon on board while the skies opened up and drenched this part of the world. I won't say it rained a lot, but when we saw animals walking toward our boat in twos being led by an old man in white robes we hauled anchor in the rain and headed south. Noah could build his own ark. Soon the sun was out and we tied to a mooring buoy at Cousteau National Underwater Park. It was still raining at the north end of the island, but warm and sunny just 10 miles south. We snorkeled the park for awhile, and then headed to the south end of Guadeloupe to anchor. That night was star-filled and beautiful, but it was still raining at the north end of the island. Now we could see why it was so green. It wasn't trees, it was mold!

We made one stop at Pointe-à-Pitre for supplies, and in the morning bid adieu to frogs in paradise. After a night anchored on the north shore of Guadeloupe we made a 30-mile motor trip back to English Harbour, Antigua to get our generator and spend the holidays. We got the generator back aboard, and for the first time in almost six months it worked. Of course it cost us another $2,200 to fix it, which made the total to repair the generator just a little over $6,700. That's $1,200 more than I paid for it in the first place, just $3\frac{1}{2}$ years ago. In that $3\frac{1}{2}$ years we have only had shore power for a total of less than six months, and we've sailed over 40,000 miles on the generator, so I won't snivel . . . yet.

Christmas in the Caribbean is a song by Jimmy Buffet, but from now on it will take on an entirely new meaning in the legend of the LOST SOUL.

It started out innocently enough. At Nelson's Dockyard they have a champagne party for all the boats. For E.C. $20 (about U.S. $7) you get an ice-cold bottle of champagne. In the heat it was as welcome as a Spandex bikini. There was a reggae band playing loud and folks were dancing everywhere.

The Lost Souls downed multiple bottles of the bubbly grape extract and soon returned to the boat. We knew we were in trouble when Jody 2, the young lady from Australia, decided to take a dip and cool off. She had her bathing suit top on and she just unbuttoned her cutoff Levi shorts and let them drop. As she straightened up she realized, as did we all, that she didn't have her bottoms on. Her recovery was excellent, as she strolled to the rail and made a perfect swan dive, leaving Shawn and I staring after her, along with most other males within eye shot.

We had Jim and Judy from GT's Pizza and Peter from La Perruche over for Christmas dinner. We had an early steak fry, and by 7 p.m. everyone was about as stuffed as the proverbial Christmas goose. Our guest went home early to sleep it off, and we all adjourned to the upper deck for a little air.

The trouble started when I felt like cooling off just after sunset, but didn't feel like getting my swimsuit on. (Me, an instigator? Never!) So I dove in as God made me. Jody 1 dove in next, then Jody 2, Kylie and Gilligan joined us. Soon we were all frolicking in the buff. Three bottles of champagne later we were all piled on the raft like a bunch of sardines, without a stitch, as the neighbors came by in their dinghy to wish us a merry Christmas. Mom and Dad got a real kick out of our frolicking, but I think the kids were a little surprised. After about three hours of slick naked bodies trying to stay on top of each other on the little six-foot round inflatable island, we all piled in the dinghy, still sans clothing, and we went and did a little caroling among the boats. You can imagine the shock as folks would come up from below deck to find one 300+ pound tattooed man, three nubile young wenches and a 25-year old surfer, all stark naked singing Christmas carols.

Needless to say we will never forget Christmas in the Caribbean, and neither will our neighbors! Once back aboard the LOST SOUL we all were down and out by 10:30 p.m. It was an early but fun-filled evening. At about 4 a.m., we all awoke at the same time to get a drink of water, and no one could remember anything except me. As I told them, slowly they started to remember. Jody 1 was so embarrassed she glowed red, Jody 2 and Kylie just kept giggling, and Gilligan sat with a glazed look on his face. Guess he's just not used to a typical LOST SOUL Christmas.

For the next couple of days we avoided our neighbors, except for those who stopped by to thank us, and we tried not to think of what New Year's eve might bring.

The day before New Year's eve the yacht JUGRA sailed in to join us. Aboard was His Royal Highness Prince Idris Shah, "the Malaysian Deck Hand" as he is known aboard the LOST SOUL, along with Captain Mark, Claire, Craig and Idris' friend and advisor, Richard.

On their arrival we invited them aboard for Jody's famous *Mud Slides* which is vodka, Bailey's and Kalua in equal portions. Idris downed five waterglass full in about two hours, and then a video was made of him being brought back aboard JUGRA and washed down with the deck hose. It was a particularly touching moment the next morning seeing him come above decks hugging his green bucket tightly to his chest, where it had resided for the night.

The next day we had an intimate New Year's eve party at Columbo's on the beach with the crew of JUGRA, the LOST SOUL and our friends Jim, Judy, Molly and Punk Rocker Alex, her date. Now close your eyes and picture this misbegotten group. One large tattooed weirdo with an entourage of three beautiful ladies, Jody, Jody and Kylie, our faithful crew Gilligan, the

Crown Prince of Malaysia, his trusty crew and very British advisor Richard, a misplaced Scotsman and his wife, a much pierced and spiked Molly and her skinhead boyfriend from England. I wonder why people were staring at us.

In any case it was a rousing success, and shortly after midnight we were joined by Pierre and Sylviane from Brussels, who would be sailing with us for the next three weeks to make a film about the weirdos on the LOST SOUL for European TV. I don't know why they wanted to film us. Isn't this a normal lifestyle?

The next day we regrouped, and at sunset went aboard the Royal Yacht JUGRA for cocktails. Once again it was an unbelievable mix of people. Just keeping track of the accents drove you nuts. There was the prince from Malaysia, his advisor from England, his captain and wife from New Zealand, our two girls from Australia, the folks from South Africa, Jim from Scotland, his wife Judy from Germany, the filmmakers from Belgium and of course the weirdos from California.

After a day of recuperating we started to load up for a day's filming around Antigua, only to find out that the camera was broken. It took awhile to get it fixed, so we had to take the day off. At the end of the day Prince Idris decided he wanted to have an intimate little dinner. He invited our crew, his crew, and assorted locals to La Perruche for dinner. A little party of 18 or so.

The royal advisor, Richard, was busily arranging the seating and placing people around the table when the waitress, who was from Jamaica, came in. She grabbed him by the arm and dragged him to his seat. "Sit down and shut up!" she said, and everyone at the table cracked up. For the rest of the evening she ran the table like it was her personal boot camp and she was the drill instructor.

By the end of the evening most of us piled into our respective dinghies for the trip home. Of course the diehards stayed out drinking. At 3 a.m. I was awakened by Kylie and Jody 2 shouting in Indonesian to JUGRA across the gap between our boats. After a few unintelligible words they slowly stripped to their G-strings, much to my pleasure since I was watching, and dove overboard. They weren't seen again aboard the LOST SOUL until the next day, when they swam home in a couple of Hard Rock Cafe shirts from Kuala Lumpur and nothing else. They wouldn't say where they had been, but Prince Idris owns the Hard Rock Cafe in Kuala Lumpur.

After everyone's head returned to a normal size, two days later, the prince and his advisor had to fly to London and back to Malaysia for a few days, and Kylie flew out on her way back to Indonesia the following day. Then Jody 2 was off to Brazil, and soon we were down to Jody, myself, Gilligan (Shawn) and Pierre and Sylviane with their ever present camera filming all this foofaraw.

Time for a Little Filming

*M*y neighbor from Redondo Beach, Jim Zietler, flew in again to sail with us for awhile. This is his fourth trip with us, and after he heard what he'd missed he was bummed he didn't come in a few days earlier.

With six people on board we headed across the channel from Antigua to Guadeloupe under full sail with a 25-knot beam wind. It was a brisk sail and the high point was getting both Pierre and Sylviane seasick at the same time. I managed it. We averaged over eight knots for the crossing, often hitting 10 and soon we were anchored once again in Day-shits, where it rained just as hard as it did the last time we were there. We motored to Cousteau National Park and spent the night, and in the morning headed down to Basse Terre to get some supplies.

After a day of rain in Guadeloupe we motored to Iles Saintes. This is a small group of islands just south of Guadeloupe. It was beautiful, but a little spendy for our tastes. After all, this is a way of life for us, and $5 for a beer is a little much. After just one day we made southward again, to the island of Dominica.

Dominica is probably the most underrated island we've had the pleasure of visiting. This place has more surprises than OJ's defense team. We anchored in the little village of Portsmouth and on the second day the filming crew, Jim, Jody and I left Shawn aboard and went on an all-day tour of the island. We visited a Carib village where the last of the Carib Indians live. These are the dudes that pissed off Columbus when he landed so he enslaved them and killed most of them. It was thought they were extinct but as it turns out there were still a few hundred left, and they were given a reservation on Dominica. We met one lady about 75 years old. We talked to her for awhile in Creole, a blend of French, Spanish and Indian. She was about 4½ feet tall and it made me feel pretty damn good that she liked me because I was so big.

Awhile later we headed over to Emerald Pool where a 50-foot waterfall falls into this clear emerald pool of river water. We were the only people and we swam under the fall and it was as if we were in the Garden of Eden.

In the morning we motored south toward Martinique. It seems the frogs have the best of the islands, except for Dominica, and they had that once and lost it. Gilligan, Jody and I had the great privileged of rebuilding the forward head, as it had taken a shit (pardon the pun, but its true!). After a few hours of machining new parts and making things fit we had it back together. We passed out of the lee of the island and set sail for a great beam reach into Martinique, seeing a green flash as the sun set and setting our hook in St. Pierre as it got too dark to see. After one night in St. Pierre we motored down to Fort-de-France to replenish the necessities and then made an afternoon crossing to St. Lucia.

St. Lucia is probably the least advertised island of the Caribbean, and that's a pity. We anchored in Rodney Bay the first night and stuffed ourselves with some great pizza at a place in the new marina, and in the morning headed south to Marigot Bay. Marigot Bay is a hidden little bay with white sand beaches, tall waving palm trees and a couple of small restaurants built right on the beach. The water is crystal clear and has more shades of blue than a Doug McLoud ballad. While we were there we were joined by about 15 other boats but it never seemed crowded. We spent the day swimming off the beach and watching Jody and Gilligan swing from a rope tied to a palm tree, and then we stopped for some afternoon cocktails. That evening a man rowed up beside our boat in a dugout with a flyer for the Shack, a small place built on stilts over the water, advertising one-inch-thick T-bone steaks. As we'd been in Europe for the past six months the thought of a thick T-bone was about as appealing as a white whale to Captain Ahab.

That night we slurped upon the finest steak ever known to man. They have them flown in from Nebraska. It was almost embarrassing as people watched Jody, Shawn, Jim and me chew the meat off the T-bone with our hands and teeth. Pierre and Sylviane tried to ignore us, but it was hard, as we were all sitting at the same table.

In the morning the film crew wanted to rent a helicopter to film the LOST SOUL under sail down island, but at dawn the rains came, so we headed south to the Pitons (two big hills that look like Madonna's nightmare bra) to await the sunshine. It never came and the helicopter had to be cancelled. I always wanted a shot of the LOST SOUL from the air. We spent the night at a small anchorage at the southern tip of St. Lucia and in the morning we headed out early to sail on the windward side of St. Vincent and into Bequia, a small island just to its south.

Bequia turned out to be even more of a dream island. We started running into old friends before we even anchored. We were hollered at by CASCADE, a 67-foot custom sloop out of San Francisco that we'd last seen a year ago on the Pacific Coast of the Baja Peninsula. As we anchored our friend Chris and Aleta whom we spent many a great night with in Puerto Rico pulled up. They'd been there for a couple of weeks and soon we had a full blown dinner party for 10, complete with a couple of the Rasta locals, that went well into the night.

It didn't take long until we were right at home in Bequia. One day we met Athneal. This dude is the only man still living that hunts the humpback whale legally. He is allowed two per year, as the people on Bequia eat the meat as well as use all the other parts of the whale. The man is 74 years old and hunts them the old fashioned way, in a 25-foot open sailboat with hand harpoon. At the entrance to his place is the jawbone of a special whale that he got over 40 years ago. It was a humpback that he got with one throw of the harpoon, straight to the heart. It is the only recorded one-thrust kill in history.

The man is amazing. He sails alongside these giants of the sea in a beautiful Bequian sailing boat and hits them with a harpoon. Then he jumps onto the whale's back and drives the hand harpoon deep into the whale between the ribs and into the heart to kill it.

We did one drift dive on the reef to about 80 feet with Chris out on the end of the island and found it to be unsurpassed in clarity and sea life. We bagged a huge lobster for our afternoon snack, and played underwater volleyball with a giant blowfish.

Getting the LOST SOUL crew out of Bequia was about as hard as prying a couple of newlyweds apart on their wedding night, but finally we had to head south again in search of even better places to make you green with envy. Our next stop would prove to be even better.

The prettiest islands in the Grenadines are the Tobago Cays. Three small islands surrounded by a reef with a billion shades of blue, and the whitest beaches you can imagine. When we arrived we went ashore for a swim and watched the sun set over the LOST SOUL, and once again I remembered why I put up with all the broken motors and systems. There is no other way to reach places like this. Once you are sitting on a beach in paradise after sailing halfway (or all the way) around the world, it just all becomes worthwhile.

Almost.

While at Tobago Cays, in the middle of paradise, the generator decided to go south one more time. The same generator that I had already had completely rebuilt just three weeks earlier, to the tune of $4,000. The same generator that had been the bane of my existence for the past six months.

We decided to head back to Bequia to try and get it fixed, again. We did a hard on sail to Mustique to stay for a day. Not just your ordinary folk live on this island. Overlooking the harbor is none other than Princess Margaret, and her neighbor is David Bowie. Down the road Raquel Welch keeps a little place, and on the north end of the island is Mick Jagger.

Of course we had to be reminded of our lowly position in life, so the mechanical gremlins kept attacking us while we were anchored there. Our refrigeration went warm, our generator went cold and our water pump went south.

I hate boats!

We sailed back to Bequia where we could get a mechanic, and soon we learned the worst. The generator that we had, until now, spent almost $7,000 repairing, had once again spit a piston.

Once again we hoisted the generator out onto a fuel dock, and we prepared to wait while the mechanics did their voodoo dance around it to make all the bad ju-ju go away. The good news was the people who did the first re-build back in Antigua were standing behind their work, and paying for the re-build. The bad news was it would take 10 days.

While we waited we figured we should make the best of a bad thing, so we kidnapped Cojo, a Rastafarian local artist, along with his girlfriend Becky from Australia and sailed over to St. Vincent to check it out. We spent two days anchored at Young Island in St. Vincent. It's a beautiful bay with two small islands that protect it from the seas and the water is crystal clear. After two days we sailed back to Bequia to pick up our generator only to find that the parts hadn't even been shipped yet, so we sat for three more days waiting.

At last the parts arrived. We had it running by 3 p.m. and at 3:15 we passed the outer harbor markings, heading toward Palm Island. We had 25 knots of wind off our back.

Palm Island is about 50 acres of white sand, palm trees, clear water and a cute little bar with cheap drinks right on the beach, which was full of topless French ladies. I guess there's one thing about frogs that I don't find obnoxious, and that is their ladies' penchant for baring their breasts.

In any case, after we pried Gilligan away from the sunbathers we hoisted that heavy chunk of iron one more time and headed to a little islet called Petit St. Vincent. This place is just like Palm Island, only smaller (about 20 acres), and it has a cute little one-acre sand bar just off its coast with a palapa type hut. As soon as we anchored behind Petit St. Vincent, Jody and I hopped in the dinghy and went out to sit on this little white piece of sand, took off our clothes and went skinny dipping.

We spent the night anchored off this little paradise under a sky filled with a moon so full you could almost see the people walking on it, and in the morning it was time to boogie south, into the land of invasions.

Grenada was about as big a surprise as finding a lawyer in heaven. We anchored in Prickly Bay (Anse aux Epines) and finally received our Christmas mail. It was mid-February and we were opening Christmas cards from all over the world. It was pretty neat, because we thought you guys all forgot about us. It cost over $165 in Fed-Ex bills just to get them to us, and we enjoyed every one of them, even if they were three months late.

As we pulled up to the dinghy dock we saw an inflatable with the name CONTRAST on it, in oriental lettering. Jody's father has been sailing the Caribbean for the past 15 years on a junk-rigged sailboat named CONTRAST. We soon learned that it wasn't her father's dinghy, but it was once, and the guy who bought it was a good friend of his. Soon we found a bunch of folks who are all friends of Jody's Dad, and it was like a reunion, only without him. We found out he was in Trinidad, where we were heading next.

The night before we ran into some folks from Hermosa Beach, where I lived for the past 20 years or so, and soon we were imbibing massive cocktails and discussing mutual friends. That night they had a huge party with Mount Gay Rum sponsoring all the rum you could drink for free. It got pretty drunk out so Jody, Jim, Shawn and a few of our friends headed out to the LOST SOUL for quieter times. Only for awhile though. Then it was back to watch the drunks, and Shawn headed out dressed in a toga for a party at the Medical school with some bimbo he'd met surfing the day before.

The following day at sunset we sailed out to cross the 80-mile channel between Grenada and Trinidad. After all, it was almost time for carnival in Trinidad, and there were already over 2,000 boats there for the party.

We missed Jody's father as he was out cruising Tobago while we were staying at the Trinidad and Tobago Yacht Club in Trinidad. The faxes we had sent him were still there, unopened, but we ran into a bunch of his friends and got to swap lies with them. We could see why a lot of folks stay in Trinidad for awhile. The prices there are unbelievable. Feed four folks for $4 and we all were stuffed. Taxis were a dollar and stocking up there was great.

I Hate Jellyfish

*I*t is a well-known fact that I hate boats, but our stay in Trinidad also made me hate jellyfish. Those cute little gelatinous critters that look like Jell-O parachutes can drive you nuts.

It seems that carnival time is jellyfish mating time. These guys float from 15 feet below up to the surface, and they cover every inch of the water. As far as the eye could see, there were these little six-inch jellyfish. Just try and run a marine engine! The damn things commit suicide in your water intakes, causing the engines, both the main and the generator, to overheat. You can't charge the batteries, you can't run the refrigeration, and the watermaker is about as useless as Dr. Ruth on a date! After the third time blowing the damn lines free, we gave up, and just let the batteries run down until we left Trinidad Harbor.

Then there are the vampire bats in Venezuela. Great! Just what we needed! It seems that there is one little thing the guidebooks don't tell you. There are these little blood-sucking critters flying around at night that think sucking people's blood is the next best thing to a chocolate shake. So we get to sleep with the windows closed and the hatches shut in 100-degree weather, and that's at night!

We headed out of Trinidad in the midst of carnival, with a million steel drums beating and more rum being spilled than even the Exxon Valdez could manage. The streets were packed and hardly a pocket went unpicked. We, of course, opted for the more sedate parties, and ended up on Main Street, Port-of-Spain, where even the criminals are scared.

Why does everyone think I'm a damn wrestler? So many

people asked me I finally started saying yes. The names "Bad Bob" and I'm on the WWF.

"Naw, it's all rehearsed."

"Only in it for the money."

By the time we left Trinidad the WWF was in big trouble!

Jim had flown out of Trinidad, so it was just Jody, Shawn and me heading to Venezuela. We had a three-day trek to get to La Cruz where we were to haulout for a long awaited bottom repair and paint.

LOST SOUL had seen more bottom than a toilet seat in the past 25,000 miles since our last haulout, so we really needed to get her out and patch her bottom. While we were there we figured we'd give her a paint job on the hull too.

We couldn't pass up the deal. The haul and bottom paint was about $600, and for just $4,000 more they said they'd paint the hull. Back home it would have been closer to $15,000, so we had to do it. A few days later we were in the CMO Marina being readied to haul our trusty boat and friend, the LOST SOUL, out of the water.

I think it was Erica Jong in her book *Fear of Flying* who said a sign of confidence was flying around the world with just a toothbrush. I have found a better test. Stand in a dirt yard in Venezuela while six Spanish-speaking counterparts of Abbott and Costello put straps around the only home you have known for the past five years, and haul it out of the water.

What, me nervous? Hell no! I always chew my fingernails from the knuckle end!

All went well, and soon we were living onboard while the boat sat in a dusty Venezuelan boatyard.

There were a few adjustments that had to be made. Like the refrigeration wouldn't work out of the water, so no more cold stuff, and the heads couldn't be used, so at night, you either climbed down a rickety old ladder the 20 feet to the ground, or you used a bucket. The thrill of awaking to 15 guys beating on the hull at dawn was also a lot of fun. Jody got the bucket duty, but she'd only dump it at night, so no one knew what she was doing.

While we were there the Bolivar, the official Venezuelan currency, devalued. We had been quoted at an exchange rate of 290 Bolivars to the dollar, and all of a sudden we were getting 360. That made for another 30% savings. For once I was starting to think I'd done the right thing. When the time came to pay for the paint job the Bolivar had dropped to almost 400 to the dollar, and in the end I paid just over $3,700 for a better job than I'd get in the States for $15,000.

We had a hard time believing the work that went into the paint job. Thirteen men worked on the boat for 10 days. First they stripped the hull and sanded it, which took three days, then they shot it with epoxy and faired it, then sanded the whole boat again. Then a coat of white Immeron two-part epoxy and more sanding, another coat with 40% clear mixed in, then more sanding, then another coat with 40% clear, then the black was shot and it looked like a new boat. The name was re-painted on the transom and on the bow, then they polished all the metal porthole rims, replaced all the below water zincs, repaired and re-fiberglassed the bottom where we'd bounced around in Panama, Belize, Florida, Greece, the Bahamas and God only knows where else, and painted the bottom with three coats of bottom paint. All in ten days, and when they were through the job was perfect.

Living in the yard actually got to be fun. Other folks had their boat also painted, people from New Zealand, Finland, Germany, Sweden and France. Each night we'd meet at the little outdoor snack bar set up near the channel and down mass quantities of brew, and then have a filet mignon dinner, for about $3.

After 11 days our friend Anita flew in from Redondo bringing needed things like cash, Crystal Light and a new American flag (our fifth had worn out, and that was all we'd brought). We splashed in the water on Saturday, did some provisioning, topped off our fuel tanks and headed for Islas Roques on the north coast of Venezuela.

The sail of 185 miles was one of the best we can recall. Twenty knots of wind off our stern blew us along at an 8-knot average for the crossing. We had planned on arriving at noon, and instead arrived at dawn.

The Numbers Game

*I*t was a night sail to Islas Los Roques. While standing night watch, I became aware that sailing is just a matter of numbers. As I sat there looking at my instrument panel I realized that I was nothing but a human calculator that processed the 16 numbers that were lit up on the panel. These 16 numbers are the difference between a good sail and pure hell. They are: 121.5, 320, 3.2, 290, 16, 2:35, 27, 25, 5.3, 11.4, 1,800, 190, 60, A340, 150, and 50.

You want to know what they mean? Here it is. The 121.5 is how many miles to the next port, and is usually about 10 miles more than you can make in daylight. 320 is the bearing to that port, and it is usually 10 degrees tighter to the wind than you can make. 3.2 is the actual speed you are making over the ground after the current (on your nose) and the wind (on your nose) slow you down. 290 is the actual course you are making against the wind and current, which are always against you. 16 is the channel on the VHF, which is driving you crazy with loud whistles (in Mexico) or other people's favorite music (in Europe) or just a lot of swearing (Spain) or a lot of stupid questions (Southern California). 2:35 a.m. is the time when I wrote all this crap. 27 is the degrees off the nose the wind is coming (my boat sails only if it is larger than 30 degrees) and 25 is the speed of the wind, directly off the nose. 5.3 is the speed through the water, before you deduct the current and drift, which are always on the nose. 11.4 is the voltage of the batteries. You only notice it when it reads that, because that is when the batteries are too low to start the boat's motor and the lights start to dim. 1,800 is where your rpms should be to charge the batteries, if only you had enough juice to start it. 190 is the water temperature, which should be at 180, so it is about to overheat and seize anyway. 60 is your oil pressure, and is always 20 PSI lower than it should be once you are at least 100 miles offshore. A340 is the course set on the autopilot to counteract the 5-knot current sweeping you into the reef off to your starboard. 150 is the bilge pump count, showing that the bilge has gone off 150 times since your last watch, and that means you have a large leak and are sinking so you won't have to worry about any of these fool numbers any more. 50 is the degrees of the water, which is usually 82 in these parts, but since the boat is sinking there will be a huge upwelling of cold water due to El Niño so at least you won't suffer too long once the fool boat goes down so you die of hypothermia before you are going under for the third time.

Any questions?

The Islas Los Roques, located about 135 miles off the coast of Venezuela, are a cruisers' paradise. A whole bunch of small white sand beaches with a million colors of blue surrounding them. The reef entrance is largely located in the mind of the man who wrote the cruising guide; after three attempts to get the LOST SOUL in through a non-existent pass we sailed a few miles north and dropped in behind it.

Once inside we anchored behind a small white sand island named Muerta and started three days of island hopping from one paradise to another, all within three to four miles of each other, and each more beautiful than the next.

At our second anchorage we ran into Craig and Mark on PANDAROSA, last seen in La Cruz, Venezuela after seeing them in Gibraltar. We anchored together for a couple of days at a few different places and met Armin and Annemarie. Annemarie is Austrian and lived in the Alps, and one night as we all had a bit too much homemade saki she gave yodeling lessons to the ladies on board. We didn't mind much, but the boats anchored near us must have thought we'd gone over the edge as the ladies howled at the moon as if they were on top of the Alps.

We soon gained our sanity, and after exploring a few of the uninhabited islands of Los Roques we caught the east wind and headed over to the Aves reefs and the island of Bonaire.

Bonaire is the land of clear water and great diving. The whole island is a dive reserve and there are over 70 moorings set for diving. We had to stay anchored in the main town and explore by dinghy and by a rent-a-van. There are also a bunch of big pink things that fly. Flamingos. Thousands of the darn things are wild all over the island.

The diving there is the best that we have found so far. Bright colored coral, hundreds of varieties of fish, water as clear as the finest aquarium and even rumors of sea horses, but we didn't spot any of those.

The town is clean and bright and for the first time in a long time we felt as if we were out of the third world. They even had a KFC joint right on the landing pier, not to mention a great bar called Karel's which had a real happy hour every afternoon.

We did a few dives with Craig and Mark and it was a real bummer to say goodbye after sailing off and on around the world with them. At sunset on March 6 we set sail from Bonaire to Curaçao and on to Aruba.

It was a good thing we took off when we did. We did an overnight sail to Aruba, where we tried to find an old friend who had moved there, but had no luck. What we did find was little America. As we entered the harbor we saw McDonald's, Pizza Hut and a Wendy's, after almost two years away from home. We'd seen a couple of McDonald's in France and

Greece, but a genuine Wendy's! Then we found a Taco Bell. Jody's favorite place on earth is Taco Bell. For the next few days it was Wendy's for lunch and Taco Bell for dinner. We had died and gone to junk food heaven.

My birthday happened to fall while we were in Aruba so that night we went to a good place for dinner. The specialty was ostrich. Pretty good too, once you get used to eating something with the texture of whale blubber.

Besides junk food there were gambling casinos everywhere, but we managed to escape almost unscathed. Maybe $40 down the tubes, but we figured we were the lucky ones.

Shawn had his brother Jim and cousin Dan fly in for the passage from Aruba to the San Blas Islands, and on to the Panama Canal. It took a little prying, but finally we got them out of the bars and into the boat, and we cast off to sail past notorious Colombia. It wasn't the drugs and pirates that we were worried about. No, it was the weather. For the past month it had been blowing 30-40 knots with seas in the 18- to 20-foot range.

As it ended up, we got very lucky. So lucky we really couldn't believe it. On the morning we left, the winds died down, and for the first day of the 575-mile passage we motored through calm winds and settling seas. On the second day we got about 15 knots of wind, and for the next 24 hours we covered 192 miles. Almost a new record for the LOST SOUL. The old record was 196 miles in 24 hours on our Pacific passage to Nuku Hiva in 1993.

It was unbelievable. The winds shifted to 120 degrees off our stern, and the seas settled even more. The third day saw partly cloudy skies and a steady 15 knots of wind. Perfect. Our five-day hell crossing had turned into one of the best four-day sail I can recall.

Now I may not have mentioned it, but Shawn, his brother, and cousin Dan, all have the same last name.

Knapp. As the passage progressed we learned that this name was quite auspicious. The family must have been named for what they do best, nap. I haven't seen people sleep so much since they invented C-Span! When not on watch, these guys made Rip Van Winkle look like an insomniac.

Of course the second day out we made a discovery. It seems that brother Jim has a tendency toward seasickness. At first he thought he was going to die. Then, a little later he was afraid he might not! That was worse. By the end of day two he looked like King Kong, strapped to the foredeck so he wouldn't fall off, and practicing for the next Olympics in the projectile spewing category. After a couple of days, when all he had left to throw up were his toenails, we took pity on him and gave him an injection of some super juice our friend Dr. Jeff gave us, and for the rest of the trip he did his best Shawn imitation. He slept. As did Cousin Dan. No doubt about it, Knapp is the ancient Greco-Roman spelling for nap, and this family perfected it.

As we were cruising, about 30 miles off the coast of Colombia we noticed a ship on the horizon. In a matter of just minutes it was bearing down on us. It was a warship. As it drew alongside we saw it was a U.S. vessel. I think it was a frigate, but I'm not really up on navy vessels. In any case, it had more guns sticking out of it than a homeboy in East Los Angeles. All of a sudden we heard our VHF.

"Sailing Vessel LOST SOUL, this is the U.S. Navy. May we speak to the skipper?"

I went over to the radio and answered them. They asked how many people were on board, if we were U.S. citizens, and if we had plans to sail closer to Colombia. I told them we hadn't planned to. He then informed us that there was a "diplomatic problem" with Colombia at the time, and he suggested, rather firmly, that we didn't approach closer than 20 miles.

This seemed a little odd, as we had heard nothing but

good from folks who had stopped in Cartagena, but since we didn't plan a stop there, it was no big deal.

A couple of weeks later, while in Panama, we found out that there was an incident between the U.S. and Colombia. By then it was all over, and was probably nothing, but it sure did seem eerie having that huge warship run us down.

Just 78 hours and 575 miles after leaving Aruba we arrived in the San Blas islands off Panama. This is the home of the Kuna indians, which are the second smallest people on earth, second only to the pygmies of Africa. These folks are so short they have to reach up to button their pants.

The place was a total surprise. I didn't have any preconceived ideas of what I'd find when we pulled in. As we did I was impressed by the sheer beauty of the place, and by the people we found there. We could hardly believe our eyes as we pulled in to anchor off Cays at the northern end of the San Blas Islands.

Brilliant blue water, crystal clear, surrounding countless small islands with white sand beaches, and deep green undergrowth, with towering palm trees. The island we anchored next to was about 150 feet across and 300 feet long, and was perfect. At the end of the beach, where the white sand was so pure it looked like sugar, it dropped off to a beautiful underwater wall of coral. The diving was not to be believed; giant crab, lobster and thousands of fish everywhere.

The first night, after we finished dinner, Jody and I grabbed our underwater lights and went for a night snorkel. At night the crabs and lobster come out to feed, and it's another world under there.

And we were alone. Not one other boat in sight. There were a couple of dugout canoes that we saw out fishing, and at night we saw fires on some of the beaches, but we didn't see any other tourists.

Of course we don't consider ourselves tourists. Since we live on our boat, we live wherever the boat happens to be, so we are travelers. A small distinction, but it allows us, at least in our own minds, not to be associated with those lily white people in the striped Bermuda shorts and flowered shirts with white sunscreen on their nose and a camera crammed in every orifice.

After a day of getting acclimatized to the easy living in San Blas we headed to a second anchorage that was even more beautiful, a blue lagoon surrounded by three small islands.

Jody and I jumped into the Zodiac tender and headed toward the beach. A palm tree grew out over the crystal clear water and the beach was white and clean. I tied the tender to the tree, and stepped back to take a photo of Jody in paradise.

A moment later Jody was looking back over my shoulder, and I turned to see what she was looking at. There stood a little boy, watching us. I smiled at him and walked over. We communicated in a little broken Spanish. His mother tongue was Kuna, but I didn't speak any. After a couple of minutes I realized that this wasn't a boy, but rather a full grown man. He was about 30 years old, but he only stood about five feet tall. His name was Yuni.

Yuni, his wife and daughter, along with his mother and father all lived here. Crystalline beaches with swaying palms and two palm frond huts right on the beach. The tallest of the family was Yuni. His mother wore a very bright colored mola dress and headdress, and had a large gold ring, right smack dab through the middle of her nose.

She couldn't have been bigger than four feet three inches but you could see she ruled the roost. They lived off the island on fish and coconuts. This is the first island group we have found where every coconut tree is privately owned, even on the uninhabited islands. You don't just pick up a coconut in this place. You ask, and, better yet, trade for them.

We gave them flour, rice, sugar and milk, and as a bonus a big jar of strawberry preserves. You should have seen their faces when they tried the preserves. They looked as if they'd won the lottery. Grins a mile wide. It made us feel pretty good, as we watched and could see the appreciation in their eyes. The little girl loved the preserves.

Awhile later the word spread that we had supplies, and soon we were surrounded by dugout canoes from the other nearby islands. We gave them all some flour, sugar, rice and milk. We'd been told while in Aruba to stock up on small packages of the staples like flour, sugar and milk. We knew we'd be in Panama in a couple of days and could get more. They were a very happy people, and I couldn't help but envy their simple way of life.

After a day of diving and swimming on crystal beaches, we headed to the next little group of islands, about ten miles away. The Chichime Cays were a little more populated and ready for cruisers like us. As we came into the lagoon we were literally surrounded by dugout canoes with whole families in them.

Unlike the lesser populated Holandes Cays, the people didn't want to barter. They wanted to sell us their molas. Molas are bright pieces of cloth sewn into artwork, and are indigenous to this area and to the Kuna people. We fended off as many dugouts as we could, but three or four managed to pull alongside and put dents in our new paint job.

When we finally got the last Kuna off the boat we went ashore to check out the island. We met a 90-year-old Kuna who had worked on the Panama Canal as a boy back in 1913. A couple of days later it was almost a pleasure to leave the overzealous people of Chichime Cays behind us, and set sail for the Panama Canal.

Once More Into the Big Ditch

The town of Colón is somewhat akin to an armed camp, with the inmates running it. As we checked Immigration we were told not to visit the streets of the city, and not to leave the Panama Canal Yacht Club grounds after dark. Sounds just like home!

Jody and I got to spend a wondrous day walking from port captain to Immigration to Panama Naval Station to admeasurers office, to scheduler and then to Customs. It's hard to believe that every boat that transits the canal has to go through all that. It took us a full day, over $300, and five hours of taxis just to get set. Then we were told we couldn't go through for three days.

Shawn's brother and cousin both had return flights to California on the day we were scheduled to go through the canal. Since they flew out of Balboa, at the other end of the canal, and we needed five people to handle lines to get through the canal, we were pretty well stuck. We tried to bribe our way through sooner but to no avail. So our crew flew out, and we started looking for some linehandlers to make the trip through the big ditch.

Meanwhile our generator, the same one we had fixed in Spain, France, Greece, Crete and Gibraltar, and had completely re-built in Antigua, and then again completely re-built in Bequia, went south on us again, and not a mechanic in sight. As we were about to enter the largest area of no fresh water for boats, Central America and Mexico, our watermaker would sit stilled, as there would be no generator to make it go.

But we were still of good cheer, because we are sailors, and all sailors are nuts! As it had rained a little each afternoon and evening (normal in the tropics), we just tied a rain catch-up to fill our tanks with rainwater.

On Sunday morning our linehandlers came aboard. "Don Juan Chong" was hired on the dock at the Panama Yacht Club and was a linehandler by profession and a former bank manager (really!). Our second linehandler was 73-year-old Lucky Leo, who lost his boat on a reef in New Guinea. He had sailed singlehanded around the world twice, and was on his third trip. I think he had been a bit too long at sea.

He had this problem. Talking. And talking. And talking some more. Before we were through the first locks everyone on board was avoiding him like a leper. But to no avail. Just when you thought it was safe you'd hear, "and then in Sumatra in 1963" from behind you and he'd be off again. Now normally we could have handled this without too much difficulty. After all, it was just to get through the canal.

But it seems that there was a hold up on the down locks, and so we were stuck in the Gatun Lake, anchored for the night, trapped with *the mouth that roared* for the whole night. If I hear the story about his falling sleep and going on the reef one more time I'll scream!

But we still needed water, so once again we hooked up our "rain preventer," and it worked. No rain. I think it's the first time in recorded history it didn't rain on Gatun Lake.

The next day our advisor was back on board at noon (he was due at 9:30, but since they are a bureaucracy they can do what they like) and we were ready to go through the last three locks.

We met our new lock partner. On the way up we were side tied with a 37-foot boat from Germany, and on the way down it should have been the same, but meanwhile this boat from France showed up. This had to be the most obnoxious Frenchman I've ever met, and there have been some doozies out here.

First of all, one of the reasons we didn't get to go through with our original crew from California was because he was in a hurry and wouldn't give up his spot. An hour later he came back down into the Colón anchorage. He didn't like the way it looked up there, so he wouldn't go through.

He showed up now while we were getting ready to descend the Pacific side. First of all he refused to side tie to go through the locks. This meant they had to add more linehandlers on the locks. We waited. He let it be known he didn't like the name of our boat, and didn't want to go down in the same lock, but they vetoed that, as the locks are 110-foot wide and 1,000-foot long and take 25 men to operate. They told him to go with us or stay in the lake.

So the German boat and the LOST SOUL raft up and get into the first lock with our lines fixed, and I look back and the frog is going nuts. He's running around like some deranged ax-murderer screaming as if he had a fish hook stuck in his scrotal sac at his linehandlers and the advisor that there's too much current in the lock. Like they could do something about it. I mean here I pulled in with seven tons tied to my side with no problem, and he was ranting that it was too dangerous.

As they started to let the water out of the lock and we started to descend he was screaming so loudly you'd have thought someone tied a knot in his colon. Everyone within a mile could hear him. Seems he didn't think his lines would be long enough.

Now Rule #1 in Panama is no one goes through without having their lines inspected by the commission, and his were 120 feet as specified, but he still thought they'd be too short and made them stop draining the lock until he could be assured it was okay.

As we pulled into the next lock he went out of control and hit the sidewall, and then yelled at his linehandlers that it was their fault. After we got out of the last lock he decided he didn't want the pilot boat to approach him and get the pilot off. He was afraid they would scratch his boat. As we left the Panama Canal we were still looking back as Froggy kept making passes by the pilot boat for the pilot to leave, but he never did come close enough, and as we drifted too far to see, he was making his fifth pass.

Back in the Pacific

━━━━━━━►◄━━━━━━━

We anchored at the first island we could find to spend the night. In the morning we started making tracks northwestward, around Punta Mala and on to Bahia Honda. It seemed odd that we had been there just 13 months ago with John, Sue, Jim and Greg, and since then had sailed well over halfway around the world *and back*.

As we arrived in the bay we were hit with a beauty of a squall, with lightning striking within a few hundred feet of us and the rain falling so thick I couldn't see the front of the boat. The good news is we got the rain preventer up, and we picked up probably 30 gallons of rainwater in our tanks.

We had dinner ashore at a small lodge started by a Vietnam vet who built the place in the middle of nowhere. The food was great, and the company even better. It's called Hannibal Lodge and the place is literally in the middle of a jungle. No roads anywhere and the only way to get in or out is by boat. As soon as you land it's like you belong there. John Morgan, the builder and operator for the last few years just sold it to a Newport Beach man, and they run it as a fishing lodge/cruisers headquarters.

At noon the next day we headed 17 miles out to an uninhabited island called Bincanco. A 50-acre jungle island with rain forest and crystal blue water and not a soul anywhere to be seen. The anchorage was perfection and at night we could hear animals that could only exist in our imaginations. Probably just some kind of mating call of a deranged beetle, but we were sure we'd stumbled onto Jurassic Park.

The following day we headed another 17 miles northwest to another island, Isla Seca, and here we found another perfect little jungle island.

Our rain preventer malfunctioned at Isla Seca. The skies opened up for a couple of hours and the three of us ran around taking rainwater showers on deck and generally making fools of ourselves.

At sunset the storm passed over and the winds shifted. We had to move out of the anchorage as we were blowing onto the shore, so we started to search for an anchorage that gave us some protection from the north wind. As there are no charts of the island it was fun feeling our way into little coves, only to find reef everywhere. Then, just to add to the fun, we ran out of fuel in tank one, and before we could get it switched over the engine died.

Now here's the deal. The boat is dead in the water with a north wind blowing us onto an uncharted reef. I have to go below into the engine room to bleed the fuel system which takes about four minutes, but seems like an hour. Then we get to start cranking the engine hoping that it starts, because if you will remember, our generator took a large poop and could only be used as a fairly efficient anchor. If the engine cranked too long the batteries would go bye-bye, and if that happened we would have no more engine until we could get to a source of electricity, which was just about as far away as the moon.

But it did start, and we soon found a secluded little anchorage between two small islets, just as the sun disappeared. The clouds dissipated as we barbecued some dead bird that the store swore was chicken, but we're more inclined to believe was very old seagull, and once again, life was beautiful.

We made a quick stop in Golfito, Costa Rica to check into the country, and spent one night at a marina with electricity, water and cable TV. By the next morning we were pulling at the lines to get away from the boob tube. We were up well into the wee hours watching movies, sports and the Playboy channel. Now I know what captive audience means. I couldn't wait to un-hitch the cable.

About seventy miles around a bend from Golfito is the Aquila de Osa Inn at Drakes Bay. We had stopped the year before to see my friend Andy who bought some property nearby, and when we arrived at the inn it was like a home-coming. We spent a couple of days there telling stories about our voyage, and one morning Jody talked me into taking a little river cruise.

There is this river that runs 15 to 20 miles into the jungle, and to enter it you have to go through some surf. The waves are breaking all the way into the mouth of the river, and they are big ones. We're talking waves of biblical proportions here. The original owner of the lodge died entering this river, and there are plenty of widows in the village that can attest to the ferocity of the entrance.

I couldn't let Jody think I was afraid, so we hopped into a panga with three people from the village and headed the three miles to the river mouth. As we approached it my heart was beating faster than a virgin's on her wedding night.

We came over the first wave, about seven feet, and surfed down it as the pilot turned on the twin 90 Johnsons full throttle. We surfed ahead of the million or so gallons of thundering water and onto the back of the one in front of it. So far, so good. Then he turns the boat abeam to the waves and looks for a hole. Just about the time my fingers left a permanent impression in the rail I was holding onto he turns it towards the river mouth and guns it again, we surf over two more waves, and I look behind me. I shouldn't have. It looked like Wiamea Bay in Maui during a surf festival.

Actually we made it in, and barely even got wet. It was then they told us that was the easy part. They said coming out was the fun part, where corpses were made.

•-•

We motored at full throttle about ten miles up the river checking out the rainforest and river life. It was beautiful and untouched. The only people we saw were an occasional fisherman, and now and then a camper on the shore. We spent an hour in a little village up river while they unloaded the empty bottles we were carrying and loaded four passengers from San Francisco who were heading for the lodge. Inwardly I grinned as I thought of the ride we had ahead of us, as we cast off and headed back down river.

As we got close to the river mouth I could barely hear the surf pounding over the beating of my heart, and as we made the last curve we saw it. It wasn't as bad as it was when we came in, but it still looked hairy. Once again our pilot, his face as calm as a preacher giving last rites, headed out into it. The new passengers just stared. Jody and I looked at each other and tried to smile, and then we were in it.

The waves were breaking and coming toward us, and just before they would hit the pilot would swerve to one side or the other to dodge the breakers, and we would ride up over the face of the wave. The front of the boat was waving like Queen Elizabeth on tour. Up one wave, slam into the next, and swerve to avoid the next.

Next time I stay on the LOST SOUL. At least I'm in control there.

Anyway, we made it. A little water in the boat, but no damage and no injuries. As I looked behind me over the breaking waves I found it hard to believe we had actually navigated it in a panga, but I'm here, so we must have.

We spent a leisurely afternoon at the lodge, and that evening at sunset we headed out for a night crossing up the coast. I remembered the little incident that occurred fourteen months earlier, as we came to Bahia Coco to check into Costa Rica. It was here I was unceremoniously thrown in the slammer with just a cockroach for company and later taken to a seedy prison by three guys with cowboy shirts and Uzi machine guns. Needless to say, I had a little anxiety as we approached the anchorage. But we had to stop, because this was also where we met Paul and Penny who run the Bohio Yacht Club, and who also used to own the Galleon restaurant in Catalina, our favorite place back in California.

We arrived at about 4 p.m. and found Paul and Penny in their apartment above the restaurant about to perform lewd and lascivious acts upon each other. Well, it's okay, they're married, and to each other, too.

We beat upon the door unmercifully until they got dressed and let us in, and then, for the next eight hours, we relived our year since we last saw them. We had a great time at their club and went to a new French restaurant for a great dinner later. Leaving the next day was hard.

We were off at dawn, heading for Bahia Elena, where a national forest was said to be the home to jaguar, pumas, ocelots and two other rare large cat families, and of course over 60 varieties of bats, Not too mention 1100 varieties of insects!

We never did find the large pussy cats, but I did manage to meet one bat (he took some blood samples from my ankle while I slept), and about 1099 of the 1100 varieties of insects. They also took some blood. I felt like I'd spent a day downtown donating blood. The bat left two neat little holes in my ankle, but the insects just supped wherever they felt like it. I figured we'd better get out of there before I started to look like Pee-Wee Herman, or worse yet, Boris Karloff!

Not to be left out, Jody got wet-eyed over a bee that decided she needed one more breast. It stung her just under her right arm and soon a lump the size of her other two protuberances started to form. It took a lot of antihistamine and about four days for her to get back down to just two.

A papagayo storm was blowing off Nicaragua as we left Costa Rica, and it was right where we wanted it, blowing out of the north-northeast at about 30 to 35 knots. We left under full sail and made great time for about four hours, and then had to reef a little as the wind and seas started to build. It looked like we might be in for a new record run, but late that night it died out, and soon we were just drifting along in a light breeze at about five knots.

But it was a night to remember. Just after a great dinner of roast beef and asparagus with hollandaise sauce we came up on deck and found the boat surrounded by hundreds of dolphins. The water had a fluorescence I hadn't seen since off the coast of Guatemala some 18 years ago while sailing on the old STONE WITCH, and wherever the dolphins dove they left a sparkling trail. It was just like a light show, and I felt like I was having a flashback from the sixties or something. Bright lights under the sea surrounded us for hours as the dolphins played in the black sea with brilliant green flashes and trails.

We also started to run into our old friends, the Guatemalan speed bumps. Some folks call them giant sea turtles, but since they became an endangered species they have been left alone, and they have gone forth and multiplied. Every fifteen minutes or so you'd see a bird sitting on what looked like a floating rock, and there would be another giant sea turtle. As we passed close our wake caught them and they did roll over and slowly flap their legs to gain their equilibrium.

If nothing else, the seas around Nicaragua, El Salvador, Honduras and Guatemala have an abundance of sea life. We've seen more porpoise and turtles here than anywhere. Probably has something to do with the viciousness of the papagayo and Tehuantepec storms that blow up to 100mph on a bad day.

As we came abreast of the Gulf of Fonseca our forward motion was subdued by a south setting current that ran as high as two and a half knots. We'd be motoring along at seven knots and be making just over four over the ground, like snails on Valium or something. It wasn't until we were off Guatemala, after passing Nicaragua, Honduras and El Salvador that the current abated. Once again we could make some time.

Oh, the birds. I almost forgot. For over 100 miles we were followed by three of the cutest looking birds. A cross between a seagull and a penguin. It flew like a seagull and looked like a penguin, and the foolish birds spent hours and hours playing some sort of game. They'd fly out away from the boat, and then, in formation, they would fly right at the hull, about three feet above the waterline, and just before hitting the boat they would put on the binders and stop in midair. They did this over and over, from before sunset one night until well into midday the next. Then they flew off.

As we approached the notorious Gulf of Tehuantepec we started to group with a few other cruisers heading north. The Tehuantepec is an area that is known for vicious storms popping up out of nowhere. It is the narrowest point in Mexico and there is a natural venturi effect when there is a high in the Gulf of Mexico that generates winds up to 100 miles per hour out of nowhere. The southern end of the Tehuantepec is Puerto Madero, and as we entered we found AZURA, ARIES II, BLUE IBIS and BITTERSWEET waiting out a storm. We joined them and waited. The afternoon of April 11 Herb on SOUTHBOUND II out of Canada broadcast on the SSB that we had a two-day window. You'd have thought they were giving away free beer across, as all of us hoisted anchor within an hour of the all clear, and as the sun set over the Tehuantepec we all went to sea. It was all clear, and the five boats kept in touch by radio all through the night, waiting to see if we'd get hit by a surprise wind. By noon the next day we knew we'd made it through the hole and a collective sigh was heard all over the Tehuantepec.

The Tehuantepec 250

————▶◀————

*T*he next day found the five-boat armada, now named *The Tehuantepec 250* (it's 250 miles across the Tehuantepec from Puerto Madero) sitting around a bunch of tables on the beach in Huatulco swapping lies about where we'd been and what we'd seen. It was almost like we were family after sharing the threat of danger. One boat was finishing a circumnavigation, one was relocating from Boston to Seattle, another was en route from England around the world, and one was like us, just out here as a way of life. It was great fun, and by the time the evening started to dwindle the twelve strangers who'd just met three days ago in Puerto Madero were friends.

The following morning BLUE IBIS and AZURA headed out at dawn, and a day later ARIES II, BITTERSWEET and the LOST SOUL followed suit. We stayed in touch on the radio, and the LOST SOUL stopped at the end of the first day in Puerto Escondido so our resident surfer, Shawn, could do some surfing. Seems that this is the fourth best surf spot in the world or something. We hoisted anchor a few days later and headed up the coast to Acapulco.

The Tehuantepec 250 participants we'd sailed north with had already arrived, as they didn't have any California surfers on board forcing a stop in Escondido. When we arrived they were all at La Marina Acapulco where my friend Alejandro resides. We'd met Alex on our previous trip through and became friends. While we had been gone he went and got married to a beautiful foxy lady, and they just had their first rugrat. Jody went ballistic when she saw the kid, and even though neither of the ladies could speak the other's language, they spent a good hour discussing God only knows what. The odd thing was it seems like they really did understand each other.

•-•

One of the northbound boats needed to get rid of some excess crew. Brian would sail with us to San Diego as crew. Little did he know what he was getting into.

We did an overnight motorsail to Zihuatanejo and anchored in the dark as the current was actually with us for a
change and pushed us in.

We spent one day hanging round Zihuatanejo and then
anchored off Isla Grande for two nights. Then, once again, it
was time for a little hell. Of course we didn't know it would be
hell, or we would have stayed at the island.

We left at dawn for a day's motoring up to a place called
Buffadero that is renown for its blowholes. This place has more
holes than a golf course and each one spurts huge quantities of
water when the seas are rolling in. And they were rolling in.

We went in to try and anchor and it looked like a scene
from Dante's Inferno. Water slashing everywhere like inside a
giant washing machine. We exercised a bit of common sense,
and headed out, and started bucking into the 20-knot headwinds. As we made our way to the west it got choppier and
more blustery.

Soon the seas were such that we felt as if we were sailing
on Xanax. Ever had one of those dreams where you are trying
to run and can't go anywhere? We saw a small spot on the chart
that said it was an anchorage, about twenty miles further up,
and we headed for it, at about 2.8 knots against the seas. As
the sun was setting we were four miles out, and we watched the
glow in the sky die as we trudged through the Jello and tried to
get in. We didn't make it. The last glow faded as we dropped
the sail and got ready to anchor by Braille.

We crept into the bay with our radar on and found we
could anchor in about 45 feet of water and it wasn't too
rough. Fortunately we couldn't see what was around us. If we
had we would've left. We spent a night with a little rock and

roll action, and at dawn saw where we were. Fifteen-foot breakers everywhere, and the rock and roll was being caused by the most humongous swells I've seen in awhile, breaking about 300 yards behind where we anchored.

At dawn we headed up the coast some more, motoring, as there wasn't enough wind to ripple the waters around us. We didn't even bother to put up a sail. We pulled into anchor the next afternoon at Cabeza Negra. Shawn and Brian hopped on their surfboards and headed to the beach, while Jody and I spent what we thought would be a leisurely afternoon on the boat.

We were wrong. The sea gods decided it was time to throw some swells at us, and a half hour after we anchored we were rockin' and rollin' like a Rolling Stones concert.

Jody and I searched the beach for the boys but they were nowhere to be seen. We'd planned to head out and sail on into Manzanillo, but instead we re-anchored a little closer to the point, and continued to rock and roll all night. At midnight they came back to the boat. It seems they met a couple of bimbos and stayed for dinner.

At dawn, we headed out towards Manzanillo, and the luxury of Las Hadas. Las Hadas is a resort that was built by a Bolivian tin magnate for himself and a few hundred of his closest friends, and was taken over by the Westin hotel chain. It's glitz, plush and decadent. In other words perfect for the LOST SOUL crew to kick back in for a few days while we waited for Pierre and Sylviane to fly in from Brussels. They're the folks shooting a video about the weirdos and the lifestyle aboard the LOST SOUL. For the next few days we rubbed elbows with the rich and famous and generally took advantage of the decadence.

Very Engaging

◄──►

*W*hen the film crew showed up we shot some stuff around the hotel, spent a lot of time by the pool and just hung out. Jody and I decided maybe we should get married.

Married? Did I say that? I guess I did, because they got it on film. It just sort of slipped out, but since Jody and I were still getting along after four years at sea we figured it might work out.

It went like this. Pierre had set up the camera on a beautiful walk beside the bay at the Las Hadas resort. Jody and I were to walk around a cascading fountain, hand-in-hand, pretending the camera wasn't there, and we were enjoying looking out at the azure blue water, with the crystal white sand beach, where our boat was anchored.

Pretend? It was beautiful. As I walked toward the water I looked at Jody and my heart melted. All I could think of was, we had sailed basically twice around the world, and now the trip was coming to an end.

After twenty years of sailing, I had finally met a partner who shared my sense of adventure and had a great attitude. I figured I either had to marry her or start paying her, as the trip was winding down, and we didn't know what was going to happen once we returned home.

So, as we walked toward the camera, all of a sudden I stopped her and turned to face her, right in front of the camera.

"Hey, Jody, let's get married." I blurted out.

"Whadaya mean?" she asked, looking as if she didn't hear me.

"You know, married, like Ozzie and Harriet." I replied.

"Whadaya mean?" she asked again.

The camera was still running, and by now Pierre and Sylviane were both looking at me like I'd lost my mind.

"Okay, do you want to get married or what?"

"Well, yeah, I guess so." She stuttered.

"Kewl!" I replied, and we turned and walked past the camera, as if it weren't there. Because, in all truth, at that moment it didn't exist. There was just the two of us, walking in paradise.

We had a little celebration at the Guadalajara Bar and Grill, and the following morning, as the cameras rolled we headed out once again into the beautiful blue Pacific.We stopped for a night in Barra de Navidad to say hello to our friend Philomena at Los Pelicanos Restaurant on the beach there. I won't say how long I've known her, but I remember her son Pablo when he was a baby, and now he's getting ready for college! Phil ran the unofficial cruisers' headquarters for western Mexico for years and we learned she'd just sold the place and was heading to the States for an operation.

On the walls of her place are the names of boats and people that have been stopping there for 25 years. I'm proud to be up there with the STONE WITCH crew in 1979, the original LOST SOUL in 1981 and 1983, my old ketch PREDATOR in 1986-1987 and the new LOST SOUL in 1995-1996.

The next day we set sail north to Tenecatita. Our first stop was at a resort on the south end of the bay, but we were told it was for members only. We went another couple miles north and anchored near a small river mouth. We spent a great day going the three to four miles up the river in the dinghy, and hanging out at the little palapa restaurant by the mouth on the beach. About five hours, 25 cervezas and six shrimp dinners later we paid the bill, a little over $20, and headed back to the boat.

That afternoon Shawn and Brian spent surfing a little way down the beach, and us old folks sipped drinks on the aft deck and watched the pelicans dive for their afternoon hors d'oeuvres.

The next day was a search for never-never land. We motored up to the anchorage at Careyes with visions of a Club Med vacation in our heads. When last we visited Careyes there was a large Club Med with hot and cold running bimbos, and the crew was looking forward to a little recreational romance. Not only was the Club Med closed for the season, but the Hotel Bel Air, where the adult crew members liked to hang out, was also out of business due to the earthquake.

Not to be deterred we headed a little farther north to a place called Paraiso, in hopes of finding some alternate form of trouble to get into. Denied! Although it was a pretty place, the northwest swells made it about as uncomfortable as Salman Rushdie at the ayatolla's hunting lodge. Once again into the breach for another hour as we headed up to Chamela. We stayed here last time and the white sand beaches and snorkeling were great. We knew it would be the same this time.

It seems that the red tide was here too, and that meant the water looked somewhat like a cesspool. We anchored for a night and headed up once more, this time to Ipala and then on to the Indian village of Yelapa. Yelapa is a very cool place that has no roads and can only be gotten to by boat. It's only 12 miles from Puerto Vallarta by sea, but a hundred years away. There are no streets, just little paths connecting the houses and stores on the mountain side above the bay, and a crystal white sand beach. Unfortunately, civilization has struck here as it did in Valdez, Alaska. An oil spill at sea had the Mexican Navy working on the beach trying to clean the tar from the sand, and picking up dead sea life while they were at it. We landed on the beach the first day and it took an hour to get the tar off our feet when we got back to the boat.

There was also a treasure hunt of sorts going on. It seems that while the navy was cleaning the beaches they stumbled on a floating bale of marijuana. They found one on the beach and started searching all the boats in the vicinity. Of course, as we were in the vicinity. . . . Do we look like drug runners or something?

Soon we were headed into Puerto Vallarta. For the next week we did as little work on the boat as possible. We tied up at Marina Vallarta where old friend Karl runs the marina. Soon we were glued to the boob tube watching cable TV like a bunch of deranged idiots, and rushing off to McDonald's for breakfast, lunch and dinner.

Ah, civilization!

*T*he first night in Marina Vallarta, Pierre, Sylviane, Jody and I had to celebrate our arrival in Puerto Vallarta, so it was off to the local bar for mass quantities of margaritas.

The following evening we finished shooting the last scenes of the video. Our mail finally arrived, and that afternoon PANDAROSA arrived in the harbor, finishing their circumnavigation of the world.

We motored the 62 miles northwest to San Blas as there was no wind. This had been the case all the way up from Panama, and we still had 1,200 miles to go.

After a rolly night in San Blas we motored up to Isla Isabella. This is one of my favorite islands and, aside from being beautiful, it also has more birds than Bill Gates has dollars and that's a lot. The film guys did some filming of the boobies and frigate birds that were nesting all over the island, and I got to play repairman on the boat.

It started when the windlass took a big poop. Without it we got to raise our anchor by hand. That's about as much fun as skinning live rhinos. I repaired the electric cable with the help of Shawn and when we were finished it was a job Mickey Mouse would be proud of.

The heavy cable leading to the windlass was run from the batteries to the windlass. We traced it for about half an hour, trying to find where it was bad. Finally we traced it to a place under the holding tank. We didn't have enough spare cable on board to replace the whole run, so we cut out a five-foot piece that was rotted, and crimped it in place using some copper tubing as electric fittings, and a pair of vice grips to crimp the ends. It worked!

Then, while tightening the fan belt on the alternator my hand slipped and water started to squirt out of the refrigeration systems heat exchanger.

Four hours later Shawn and I finished making a truly Rube Goldberg replacement for it, but it worked. Then the expansion valve in the reefer took a big poop.

A few hours later I had replaced the bad valve and recharged the system. It didn't work well, but it worked enough to cool the beer.

We noticed the forward running lights were on, and the switch was off. I got to play follow the wire for the next few hours.

As we approached Mazatlán it was almost an anti-climax when the bilge pump stuck on, and we found that the relay switch had taken a large poop. It was soon bypassed and the excess amounts of water that flowed from our aging packing gland was once again pumped back into the sea where it belonged.

We arrived at the new Mazatlán marina and found a heaven for boaters. The first two days were free, and we were only staying three days.

While there we did a crew shuffle. We shipped Brian off to Arizona with a sore throat, threw Pierre and Sylviane forcibly onto a plane (it was freezing and raining in Brussels and they didn't want to go!) and loaded Tom and Vicki, both from the South Bay area of South California, onto the boat.

The first night we went out for dinner with the whole gang. When they started to hand out the free poppers, Tom couldn't say no. A popper is a double shot of tequila with a drop of Seven Up which is slammed on the table and forced down the throat of unsuspecting gringos. This is the way Mexico gets back at us for taking Texas.

By one a.m. "Fall Down" Tom had earned his nickname

the hardway. He fell down in the disco, he fell down in the street, he fell down in the cab and had to be dragged down the dock onto the boat, where he fell down on deck and spent the night, half on and half off the aft storage box.

We woke him the next morning with John Phillip Sousa's rendition of *Stars and Stripes Forever* at full blast on the outdoor speakers of the boat. When his eyes slammed open and he jerked upright to smack his head on the mizzen boom he was greeted with a fresh shot of tequila. The following day we took pity on him and let him sleep it off.

About midday, our new crewmember, Vicki, showed up. As it turns out this was a very auspicious day. A couple of years later Vicki would become the Associate Publisher on the Magazine *Latitudes & Attitudes*, which I started at the end of the voyage.

But first it was time to sail to Cabo. I mean we sailed to Cabo. Not motored like we've done most of the trip up from Panama. We actually put up those big white pieces of cloth and the wind filled them and we turned off the engine.

After a great sail of about 185 miles we pulled into Cabo San Lucas. Cabo is like our home away from home and we were busier than a Girl Scout leader whose troop had gone into a biker bar. We hung out Mike Grazenich's Latitude 22 most of the time. He's an old riding partner who now looks like Jerry Garcia, only Mike's still living (we think!).We met some new folks during one of our nightly forays into the deep mists of Cabo's nightlife, and spent our last day on the boat sitting around discussing the different way of life in Tulsa and Kansas City.

An old friend from Redondo showed up in the form of Lester the Molester, who was now living in Cabo, so we signed him on as additional crew, gave poor Vicki to Mike as a going away present, and once again, in the morning we headed north.

They call the trip up the Baja Peninsula the "Baja Bash"

and there is a good reason for that. As we rounded the tip of the Baja we were hit right smack dab in the snout with 30 knots of wind and rough seas. We were slammed down like an unwanted stepchild to where we could only make about two knots, and for the next 36 hours we beat into winds that would make most boaters prefer the coal mines of central Pennsylvania as a way of life.

Unfortunately some four days later as we sat in the third anchorage in as many days, we watched the wind meter spin at about 25 to 30 knots and waited for a lull. Each day we would slam into the seas and winds like some demented scene out of the old *Victory at Sea* intro. Water over the bows became a way of life, and the salt spray coated the whole boat like a sugar cookie. Not only that, but the water got cold. The 90-degree waters of Panama became 80-degree waters in Mexico, but we could live with that. As soon as we rounded the tip of Cabo the water got colder than a well digger's derrière. Like in the low 50s.

So here we were, getting beat to death with ice cold water splashing over us, making no speed at all, and burning fuel like it was free, and all this to get back to Redondo Beach. It would have been easier to go back to Tahiti.

After a week of bashing headlong into heavy seas and winds it started to subside as we got to within a hundred miles of San Diego. Even if we didn't have a chart to tell us we were getting closer to the U.S., the idiotic chatter on the VHF radio could have told us. I think the height of dunderheadism was this anal retentive clod who came onto the VHF radio calling "Coast Guard! Coast Guard!" When both the San Diego and Long Beach Coast Guard stations came on the radio to help with the life and death struggle he was going through, he explained that he was having trouble with his cellular phone, and wanted them to help him make a call.

•-•

We stayed a last night anchored in the Coronado Islands just 14 miles from San Diego Bay. It seemed strange sitting there having dinner looking across at the multi-million lights of California.

Once in San Diego it was like old home week. As we tied up at the Kona Kai Club my friend of 20 years, Billy Jack, was waiting on the dock. He'd seen us come in. While we were saying hello, Marty Fogel, who'd lived across the dock from me in Redondo some 20 years ago, pulled in with his dinghy to say he saw us come in and had just moved down. As we were having breakfast the next morning we ran into Jack who was overseeing the rebuild of a 1930s schooner for our friend Ted. We'd met the two of them in Cabo four years ago, again in Cabo two years ago, and they had flown in from Vegas for my fiftieth birthday a few years back.

Later that day Karl, the marina manager from Puerto Vallarta showed up bringing us copies of a two-part article that was done about us when we were in Vallarta. It was almost like being home, yet we were still two weeks from our real homecoming in Redondo.

For the next two weeks we were busy as we tried to get our varnish back into shape and entertained a bunch of folks who came down from Los Angeles.

Every day someone would come down, or we'd bump into old cruising friends, and not once in the two weeks did Jody and I have an hour to ourselves. We did manage to get to the zoo and Sea World, but only because friend Neil kidnapped us.

While in San Diego Diesel Dan tried to get the generator running for us, but it was toast. After dumping over $7,000 into trying to keep it going, in the end it was as about as useless as ears to a punk rock drummer. He pulled it out and said he'd take it home and sell it to someone, sending us the money he'd get for it. We never saw or heard from him again.

All too fast it was time for us to head towards Redondo. We set sail just before dawn from San Diego and headed towards Catalina, where we have started and finished the last four voyages, at Twin Harbors. The 80-mile sail to Avalon Harbor was idyllic with a 10-knot breeze off our stern, and it was only through the strongest will power that we didn't just set the autopilot a few degrees to the west, and head straight to Hawaii. Of course if we'd done that we wouldn't be able to piss off all our friends at home, so we shrugged our shoulders, grinned at each other for a few minutes, and then sailed on to Catalina.

As we started to come into Avalon we decided we wanted our last days at sea to be a little less "citified" so we turned out of the city's harbor and headed up-island to a little anchorage I knew around the other side of Long Point. Just as we were starting to drop our anchor we heard LOST SOUL being hailed on the VHF radio. It was Jill and Curt on NAMAHANA, and they'd come out to welcome us. Saying goodbye to our last night at sea alone, we kept the anchor on board and headed the last few miles into Twin Harbors. This is where we always start and stop our expeditions. When we picked up the mooring we could see the lights of Redondo Beach 24 miles across the Catalina channel. As NAMAHANA pulled in beside us I knew the trip was over. We were home.

In the previous five years Jody and I had sailed over 50,000 miles and visited 50 countries. We had anchored in over 300 different anchorages and stopped at 150 islands. In that time we had a dozen different crew people, 40 guests and used over 22 mechanics who spoke six languages other than English. We shot over 3,500 35 mm slides and 30 hours of video.

And after two days in civilization we realized we could never stay for long and started to plan our next adventure.